M000236953

LANGUAGE ARTS
INSTANT ASSESSMENTS
for Data Tracking
Grade 5

Credits
Author: Redeana Davis Smith

Visit *carsondellosa.com* for correlations to Common Core, state, national, and Canadian provincial standards.

Carson-Dellosa Publishing, LLC
PO Box 35665
Greensboro, NC 27425 USA
carsondellosa.com

978-1-4838-3620-1
01-339161151

Table of Contents

✦ Assessment and Data Tracking ✦

Data tracking is an essential element in modern classrooms. Teachers are often required to capture student learning through both formative and summative assessments. They then must use the results to guide teaching, remediation, and lesson planning and provide feedback to students, parents, and administrators. Because time is always at a premium in the classroom, it is vital that teachers have the assessments they need at their fingertips. The assessments need to be suited to the skill being assessed as well as adapted to the stage in the learning process. This is true for an informal checkup at the end of a lesson or a formal assessment at the end of a unit.

This book will provide the tools and assessments needed to determine your students' level of mastery throughout the school year. The assessments are both formal and informal and include a variety of formats—pretests and posttests, flash cards, prompt cards, traditional tests, and exit tickets. Often, there are several assessment options for a single skill or concept to allow you the greatest flexibility when assessing understanding. Simply select the assessment that best fits your needs, or use them all to create a comprehensive set of assessments for before, during, and after learning.

Incorporate Instant Assessments into your daily plans to streamline the data-tracking process and keep the focus on student mastery and growth.

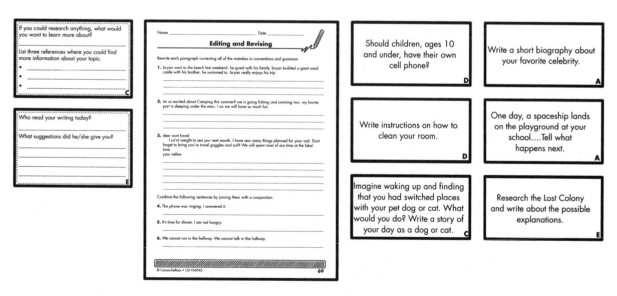

A variety of instant assessments for writing

Types of Assessment

Assessment usually has a negative association because it brings to mind tedious pencil-and-paper tests and grading. However, it can take on many different forms and be a positive, integral part of the year. Not all assessments need to be formal, nor do they all need to be graded. Choose the type of assessment to use based on the information you need to gather. Then, you can decide if or how it should be graded.

	What Does It Look Like?	**Examples**
Formative Assessment	• occurs during learning • is administered frequently • is usually informal and not graded • identifies areas of improvement • provides immediate feedback so a student can make adjustments promptly, if needed • allows teachers to rethink strategies, lesson content, etc., based on current student performance • is process-focused • has the most impact on a student's performance	• in-class observations • exit tickets • reflections and journaling • homework • student-teacher conferences • student self-evaluations
Interim Assessment	• occurs occasionally • is more formal and usually graded • feedback is not immediate, though still fairly quick • helps teachers identify gaps in teaching and areas for remediation • often includes performance assessments, which are individualized, authentic, and performance-based in order to evaluate higher-level thinking skills	• in-class observations • exit tickets • reflections and journaling • homework • student-teacher conferences • student self-evaluations
Summative Assessment	• occurs once learning is considered complete • the information is used by the teacher and school for broader purposes • takes time to return a grade or score • can be used to compare a student's performance to others • is product-focused • has the least impact on a student's performance since there are few or no opportunities for retesting	• cumulative projects • final portfolios • quarterly testing • end-of-the-year testing • standardized testing

The assessments in this book follow a few different formats, depending on the skill or concept being assessed. Use the descriptions below to familiarize yourself with each unique format and get the most out of Instant Assessments all year long.

Show What You Know

Most anchors begin with two *Show What You Know* tests. They follow the same format with the same types of questions, so they can be used as a pretest and posttest that can be directly compared to show growth. Or, use one as a test at the end of a unit and use the second version as a retest for students after remediation.

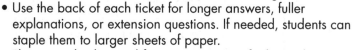

Exit Tickets

Most anchors end with exit tickets that cover the variety of concepts within the anchor. Exit tickets are very targeted questions designed to assess understanding of specific skills, so they are ideal formative assessments to use at the end of a lesson. Exit tickets do not have space for student names, allowing teachers to gather information on the entire class without placing pressure on individual students. If desired, have students write their names or initials on the back of the tickets. Other uses for exit tickets include the following:

- Use the back of each ticket for longer answers, fuller explanations, or extension questions. If needed, students can staple them to larger sheets of paper.
- They can also be used for warm-ups or to find out what students know before a lesson.
- Use the generic exit tickets on pages 7 and 8 for any concept you want to assess. Be sure to fill in any blanks before copying.
- Laminate them and place them in a language arts center as task cards.
- Use them to play Scoot or a similar review game at the end of a unit.
- Choose several to create a targeted assessment for a skill or set of skills.

Word Lists

Word lists consist of several collections of grade-appropriate words in areas that students need to be assessed in, such as sight words, spelling patterns, and words with affixes. They are not comprehensive but are intended to make creating your own assessments simpler. Use the word lists to create vocabulary tests, word decoding fluency tests, spelling lists, etc., for the year.

Cards

Use the cards as prompts for one-on-one conferencing. Simply copy the cards, cut them apart, and follow the directions preceding each set of cards. Use the lettering to keep track of which cards a student has interacted with.

- Copy on card stock and/or laminate for durability.
- Punch holes in the top left corners and place the cards on a book ring to make them easily accessible.
- Copy the sets on different colors of paper to keep them easily separated or to distinguish different sections within a set of cards.
- Easily differentiate by using different amounts or levels of cards to assess a student.
- Write the answers on the backs of cards to create self-checking flash cards.
- Place them in a language arts center as task cards or matching activities.
- Use them to play Scoot or a similar review game at the end of a unit.

Assessment Pages

The reproducible assessment pages are intended for use as a standard test of a skill. Use them in conjunction with other types of assessment to get a full picture of a student's level of understanding. They can also be used for review or homework.

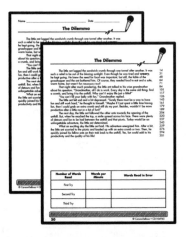

Fluency Pages

Use the paired fluency pages to assess students' oral reading fluency. Provide a copy of the student page to the student, and use the teacher copy to track how far the student read, which words he or she struggled with, and the student's performance on repeated readings. The word count is provided at the end of each line for easy totaling. Then, use the related comprehension questions to assess the student's understanding of what he or she read.

Exit Tickets

Exit tickets are a useful formative assessment tool that you can easily work into your day. You can choose to use a single exit ticket at the end of the day or at the end of each lesson. Simply choose a ticket below and make one copy for each student. Then, have students complete the prompt and present them to you as their ticket out of the door. Use the student responses to gauge overall learning, create small remediation groups, or target areas for reteaching. A blank exit ticket is included on page 8 so you can create your own exit tickets as well.

What stuck with you today?

_____

_____

_____

_____

_____

List three facts you learned today. Put them in order from most important to least important.

1. _____

_____

2. _____

_____

3. _____

_____

The first thing I'll tell my family about today is

_____

_____

_____

_____

_____ .

The most important thing I learned today is

_____

_____

_____

_____

_____

_____ .

Color the face that shows how you feel about understanding today's lesson.

☺ 😐 ☹

Explain why. _____

_____

_____

Summarize today's lesson in 10 words or less.

_____

_____

_____

_____

_____

One example of _____

is _____

_____

_____

_____

_____ .

One question I still have is _____

_____

_____

_____

_____

_____ .

How will understanding _____

_____

help you in real life? _____

_____

_____

_____

_____

One new word I learned today is

_____ .

It means _____

_____

_____

_____ .

Draw a picture related to the lesson. Add a caption.

_____

_____

If today's lesson were a song, the title would

be _____

_____

because _____

_____

_____ .

The answer is _____ .

What is the question? _____

_____

_____

_____

_____

✦ Show What You Know ✦

Reading: Literature

Read the story. Then, answer the questions.

My Big Moment

We double-checked the amp volume before I sat down on the stool Candice had set out for me. Erin sat down on a stool to my left, and I looked down at my hands. Although this was a big event, I couldn't figure out why I was so nervous. I had rehearsed this at least a thousand times. I took a deep breath to calm the butterflies in my stomach and nodded to Erin. She smiled and began to strum the first chords. I closed my eyes and joined in to start the first verse. After a few moments, Caitlin began to sing. My hands were sweating, and I had to concentrate to keep my breathing even. I worried my fingers would slip and mess up the chords, but I kept playing anyway. Before I knew it, I realized the song was almost over, so I opened my eyes and looked up. The audience was smiling and I found myself smiling too. Many people were even tapping their toes with the beat that we were strumming. Caitlin finished her last **note**, and our final chords died away. After our performance, Candice thanked me and said she thought our song was perfect.

1. What was the narrator doing?

_____

_____

2. What clue best reveals what the narrator was doing?

   A. "We double-checked the amp volume . . ."

   B. "My hands were sweating, and I had to concentrate to keep my breathing even."

   C. "I worried my fingers would slip and mess up the chords, but I kept playing anyway."

   D. "Erin sat down on a stool to my left, and I looked down at my hands."

3. Which statement best describes Erin's attitude?

   A. Erin is calmer than the narrator.

   B. Erin is more nervous than the narrator.

   C. Erin is glad to be playing guitar instead of singing.

   D. Erin in not happy.

4. How would this story be different if Candice were the narrator?

   A. The reader would not know that the audience enjoyed the song.

   B. The reader would not know that the narrator is very nervous.

   C. The reader would not know that Erin played guitar.

   D. The reader would not know that Candice liked the song.

5. What type of figurative language does the author use when the narrator states she has butterflies in her stomach? _____

What does the author mean by this? _____

_____

_____

_____

6. What point of view is used in this story?

A. first person   B. second person

C. third person   D. fourth person

7. How might the narrator approach her next opportunity to do something that makes her

nervous? _____

_____

8. What is the theme of this passage? _____

Explain. _____

_____

_____

9. How do you think the narrator's feelings change from the beginning of the passage to the end? Use details from the story to support your answer.

_____

_____

_____

10. In the text, **note** means which of the following?

A. a short letter   B. a reminder

C. a single tone   D. to pay attention to

Name _____   Date _____

Show What You Know
Reading: Literature

Read the story. Then, answer the questions.

Animal Lovers

Terrance and Tabitha had always loved animals. Even as young children, the twins would rescue hurt or lost creatures they found on the farm. They learned to take care of animals from their parents and the farm veterinarian. As they grew older, they continued to rescue animals, often housing them in their parents' barn until a home could be found. By the time the twins were ready to graduate from high school, the O'Kelley twins had rescued over 100 dogs, even more cats and kittens, and an assortment of birds and other animals.

Mr. and Mrs. O'Kelley were not exactly surprised when the twins came to them with a new and wonderful scheme.

"Tabitha and I would like to open a pet rescue shelter," said Terrance. "We will take in stray animals and try to find their owners. If we can't, we will find them good homes. We'd like to use the empty side of the main barn. We have it all planned out."

"How will you afford to feed and care for these animals?" Mrs. O'Kelley asked.

"We plan to ask local pet shops and individuals to donate pet food," Tabitha explained. "We also plan to collect cans for recycling."

"And new pet owners will pay an adoption fee that will help cover some of the costs of caring for their new pets," said Terrance.

"But, what about school?" Mr. O'Kelley questioned. "You'll both be going to college in the fall."

"We know, but we're going to college in town," Tabitha replied. "We'll be close by, and we'll care for the animals after classes."

Dad had another question. "What about the animals that really need medical attention? How do you plan on paying Dr. Wong for checking them out? Taking in sick or injured animals can be dangerous, kids!"

"Dr. Wong agreed that this is a great idea. He's even willing to volunteer two hours a week if we help him on Saturday mornings. All we have to do is clean out the four kennels he has at the office. We know how to do that since we do it for our own animals, so it won't be a problem," explained Tabitha.

Mr. and Mrs. O'Kelley looked at each other. Mom smiled and said, "Well, you two certainly have done your homework!"

Dad said, "If we let you try this, it's on a trial basis only, just for the summer months. Also, you cannot have more than six '**residents**' at a time."

"We won't let you down," Tabitha promised. "We won't let the animals down, either," said Terrance. The twins were tinkled pink!

1. What will happen if Terrance and Tabitha do a good job taking care of the animals all summer?

    A. Their parents will allow them to keep using the barn.

    B. Dr. Wong will give them full-time jobs.

    C. They will not take in any more stray animals.

    D. Their parents will buy them a building in town for their rescue shelter.

2. Is this story told in first person, second person, or third person? _____

3. Why did Tabitha and Terrance think starting an animal rescue would be a good idea? Use details from the text to support your answer.

_____

_____

4. What does Mr. O'Kelley mean by **residents**?

    A. volunteers   B. rescued animals

    C. potential pet owners   D. veterinarians

5. Who is Dr. Wong? Use details from the text to support your answer. _____

_____

6. Why is the information in the first paragraph important?

    A. It shows that rescue centers are difficult to manage.

    B. It shows that Terrance and Tabitha do everything together.

    C. It shows that Terrance and Tabitha will be good at running the rescue center.

    D. It shows that Terrance and Tabitha have little experience with animals.

7. In the text, "tickled pink" is what type of figurative language? _____
What does it mean? Use details from the story to support your answer.

_____

_____

8. What is a possible theme of this passage? Use details to support your answer.

_____

_____

_____

9. Based on the passage, how would you describe Terrance and Tabitha? Use details from the text
to support your answer. _____

_____

Making Inferences

Use these cards to assess students' general understanding of making inferences. Teachers can quickly use the cards to assess a student one-on-one. Students could also work individually or in pairs to answer all cards. Have students support their answers for a more in-depth understanding of their inferencing skills. To use the cards as a formative assessment, read a card aloud and have students respond on whiteboards for a quick check of understanding inferences. As students progress with the skill, students could create their own cards to add to the deck.

Nina and Carlos woke up late and missed the bus. Luckily, their mom dropped them off and they arrived just as the bell was ringing. Where were Nina and Carlos going? **A**	When I entered the building, it was very quiet. There were people walking around looking at the books on the shelves. People were also sitting at tables reading. Where am I? **B**
Mom packed the tent, sleeping bags, pillows, marshmallows, flashlights, and firewood in the back of the van. It was going to be a great weekend! Where is the family going? **C**	My grandfather and I went to the hardware store to pick up one more pack of seeds. We have the shovel, hoe, and water hose ready to go. What am I doing with my grandfather today? **D**
I smiled as I looked around the room at family, friends, balloons, and presents. I blew out my candles and made my wish. Where am I? **E**	According to my list, we didn't need anything on aisle 3 so I sent the boys to aisle 4 to get tomato sauce, pasta, and beans. Then, we would be ready to check out. Where am I? **F**

She told me that I didn't have a fever after she took my temperature, but my throat was red and swollen. She prescribed some medicine to pick up at the pharmacy.

Where am I?

G

The family had seen so many animals already today. But they were most excited about the polar bears, giraffes, and monkeys. According to their map, those were the next three exhibits.

Where is the family?

H

John clapped and yelled for his team when he heard the ball hit the bat and sail into the stands.

Where is John?

I

She laid out all of the ingredients first. Then she followed the directions step by step and placed the pan in the oven. When the timer went off, the house was already filled with the delicious sweet aroma.

What is she doing?

J

The class lined up at the door. The two helpers grabbed the tub full of balls and jump ropes.

Where was the class going?

K

Finally, the day had come! After applying sunscreen, the two friends walked to the edge, held their breath, and jumped in.

What are they doing?

L

After a loud pop, Toby carefully drove the car to the side of the road. He got out to look. It was a good thing he had a jack and a spare in the trunk.

What happened to Toby's car?

M

She walked through the classroom door and saw it on her desk. She was nervous but glad she spent her extra time over the weekend studying.

What is she doing?

N

Making Inferences

Read the story. Use context clues to infer the answers to the questions.

The Audition

Hayley's heart thudded as she took her place in the registration line. When she reached the front, a woman handed her an application. Hayley completed it, leaving the section marked *Experience* empty.

Applicants crowded the lobby—chatting, laughing, and stretching their muscles. Some girls wore dance attire. Hayley felt awkward in her simple T-shirt and shorts. Her stomach twisted from nerves.

She nearly vaulted out of her seat when someone tapped on her shoulder. "Hi, Hayley! Trying out for the production?"

Hayley nodded. She recognized the girl as Roxanne from geography class.

"The dance portion of the audition will be difficult in those flip-flops. Did you bring a pair of character shoes?"

"What are character shoes?" Hayley asked.

Roxanne smiled sympathetically. "I have an extra pair of jazz sneakers in my backpack. They are flexible, and I think they will fit."

"Thank you. I must have amateur emblazoned on my forehead. I probably shouldn't audition, but I love singing."

Roxanne's grin lit up her face. "We are all amateurs, and it is fantastic! The choreographer will conduct the dance audition after the vocal audition. I looked at the schedule. You audition right before me! Have you marked 16 bars on your music?"

"What do you mean by 16 bars?"

Roxanne reached for the sheet music in Hayley's hand. "You need to sing 16 measures of music from your audition piece. If the director likes your voice, he might ask you to sing more. You should try these ones." Roxanne marked the page and tilted her head. "They just called your number!"

Hayley checked the paper in front of her. She gulped. "Break a leg," Roxanne said. "What?" "It means 'good luck!'" Roxanne pushed Hayley up to the stage. Hayley's legs were shaking so hard that she wondered if they would shatter. She handed her sheet music to the accompanist, but she was nervous about singing with a piano. She'd never done it before. Luckily, after a couple of bars she lost herself in the music. She almost forgot to stop! A man in the audience clapped. "That was very nice. Would you please sing a little more?"

Hayley grinned. "Absolutely!"

1. Is this Hayley's first time auditioning for a show? Explain. _____

_____

2. Is this Roxanne's first time auditioning for a show? Explain. _____

_____

3. Has Hayley had dance training? Explain. _____

_____

Name _____ Date _____

Making Inferences

Read the story. Then, answer the questions.

In Line for a License

"Come on, Mom!" Peter urged. He practically dragged her through the revolving front doors. They made their way toward a room with a sign that read "Department of Motor Vehicles."

Once inside the room, Peter completed some paperwork. Then, he joined a long line of people. They were waiting their turn at the counter. As Peter waited, he stared at a poster on the wall. It read, "You must be at least 16 to apply for a license."

As Peter moved forward, he **peppered** his mom with questions. "You'll let me have the keys right away, won't you?" he asked. "It's all right if I take it out tonight, isn't it? I'll fill up the tank, I promise."

An hour later, Peter raced out of the building with a huge grin on his face. His success was evident. "Come on, Mom!" he called. "Your driver is ready to take you home!"

1. When Peter first enters the building, he feels

    A. agitated.   B. relieved.

    C. impatient.   D. angry.

2. Where is Peter? Why is Peter here? _____
List three clues that helped you come to that conclusion.

    A. _____

    B. _____

    C. _____

3. Based on the story, what does the word **peppered** mean?

    A. asked rapidly   B. spice

    C. shower with   D. argued with

4. To what keys is Peter referring? Explain how you know. _____

_____

5. Describe how Peter felt upon leaving the building and why. _____

_____

_____

Name _____   Date _____

Making Inferences

Read the poem. Then, answer the questions.

Smack

His knees knocked as he stepped up to the plate,
All he wanted to do was hit it clear to the gate.

But last time he was here, he swung not once, not twice
But three times for air and his team paid the price.

This time, he hoped for more but he watched the ball zip by
Not once, but twice. Third time he swung and let out a cry.

Smack went the bat. Flying went the ball. Cheers from the stands.
Around he ran to home with high fives into all his teammates' hands.

1. What is the poem about? Explain how you know. _____

_____

2. In line 1, what does "his knees knocked" mean? Explain how you know.

_____

_____

3. Compare how you think the narrator felt at the beginning of the poem compared to the end of

the poem. _____

_____

4. In line 4, what does "paid the price" mean? Explain. _____

_____

_____

5. Write a different title for this poem. _____
Why do you think it is a good title?

_____

_____

Name _____ Date _____

Theme Matching

Stories often include a theme. Match the common themes to their messages.

| acceptance | courage | perseverance | cooperation | hope |
| compassion | honesty | friendship | preparedness | kindness |

_____ **1.** Characters find that it is always best to tell the truth no matter what.

_____ **2.** Characters work together to solve a problem or achieve a goal.

_____ **3.** Characters show strength to overcome a fear or accept a risk.

_____ **4.** Characters respect and accept others' differences and beliefs.

_____ **5.** Characters continue to believe even when facing difficult times.

_____ **6.** Characters are friendly, generous, and considerate of others.

_____ **7.** Characters trust each other and never turn their backs on their friends.

_____ **8.** Characters want to make those who are suffering feel better.

_____ **9.** Characters avoid trouble by being prepared and ready for any situation.

_____ **10.** Characters work hard and it pays off in the end.

Understanding Theme

Read the passage. Then, answer the questions.

The Test

There was going to be a test on Friday covering the meteorology unit. Ethan was determined to get at least 95 percent on the test. He had to get an A in science on his report card. Grades were important to Ethan. He had several days to prepare, so he knew he could do it if he studied hard.

On Monday, Ethan made study cards with all of the vocabulary words and definitions he needed to know. That evening, he took the cards with him and reviewed them as his mom drove him to soccer practice. The next day, he made an outline of the unit. His dad quizzed him from the outline. On Wednesday, his friend Zach came home with him after school. They each made 25 game cards with questions from the unit. The boys kept track of the number of questions they each answered correctly. Ethan got the most correct; his hard work was paying off! Ethan went to his room on Thursday evening and studied quietly for an hour. The next day, he confidently answered every question on the test. He knew he had done well. When his teacher passed back the tests at the end of the day, Ethan smiled with pride. He had **exceeded** his goal. He scored 100 percent on the test!

1. What is the theme of the passage?

    A. hard work pays off

    B. good grades are important

    C. meteorology is a difficult subject

    D. success comes from working together

2. What information from the passage supports the theme? Circle all of the answers that apply.

    A. There was going to be a test.

    B. He knew he could do it if he studied hard.

    C. He scored 100 percent on the test.

    D. His friend Zach came home with him.

3. How did the author structure this passage?

    A. cause/effect   B. problem/solution

    C. chronologically (time order)   D. compare/contrast

4. Based on the passage, what does **exceeded** mean? Use details from the story to support your answer.

_____

_____

Understanding Theme

Read the poem. Then, answer the questions.

Progress

March
Bounce, dribble, drop, roll
Bounce, dribble, shoot
Nowhere even close to the goal

April
Bounce, dribble, dribble, drop, roll
Bounce, bounce, dribble, shoot
A little bit closer to the goal

May
Bounce, bounce, dribble, dribble
Bounce, dribble, dribble, shoot
Grazed the rim of the goal

June
Bounce, dribble, dribble, dribble
Shoot, shoot, shoot
Swish, straight in the goal

1. What is the theme of the poem? _____

2. Use details from the text to explain why you chose that theme.

_____

_____

3. In the poem, what does the word **grazed** mean? Use details from the text to support your answer.

_____

_____

4. Follow the structure of the poem and write your own stanza for February or July.

_____

_____

_____

Comparing and Contrasting

Read the passage. Compare and contrast the two characters. Then, answer the questions.

Two Talents

Brayden and Reid were next-door neighbors and in the same class at school. Brayden was probably the brightest, most studious student in the class. Reid was definitely the best, most dominant athlete in the school. The boys often carpooled to school. But, in the afternoon, they came home separately. Reid usually stayed and played basketball with some of the other boys. He was very competitive and enjoyed winning. Brayden usually went straight home and did his homework and then read a book. He was diligent and took pride in his academic achievements.

One day after school, Brayden asked Reid if he could stay and play basketball with him and the other boys.

"No way! Do you even know how to play basketball?" Reid scoffed as he headed to the court. Brayden was hurt. He went home and studied for the science test.

The next day when Brayden and Reid got to the classroom, their teacher passed out the science test. Everything on the test was material Brayden had studied, so he had no trouble answering the questions. When Brayden had finished, he noticed that Reid had barely written anything on his test. Later, when the tests were returned, Brayden received a 100 at the top of his paper. Reid had a note written on his test saying he must take the test again.

After school, Brayden offered to help Reid study for the test. Reid gratefully accepted the help even though he was a little embarrassed at how he had treated Brayden the day before. The next day, Reid passed his science test. He thanked Brayden for his help and asked him if he could return the favor by teaching Brayden how to play basketball. Brayden gladly accepted the invitation.

1. How are the boys alike? _____

_____

2. How are the boys different? _____

_____

3. Write the words and phrases that are used to describe each boy in the passage.

A. Brayden _____

B. Reid _____

4. How did Reid's feelings toward Brayden change from the beginning of the story to the end? Underline the details from the text to support your answer.

_____

_____

Comparing and Contrasting

Read the journal entries. Then, answer the questions.

Camp Journal

Day 1

I wanted to jump back in my mom's van the moment she dropped me off this morning. Why couldn't I have just stayed with my aunt like last summer? I do not know a single person here. My cabinmate arrived before me and took the bottom bunk. I have never slept on the top bunk before. It is so high up and I'm scared I'm going to fall off. My flashlight is about to run out of batteries and I didn't bring any extras. I guess I'll try to sleep now. Only 13 more days.

Day 14

I'm so sad that camp ends tomorrow. I have had the absolute best time meeting new people and learning new things. The zip line and ropes course were my favorite! My friends just stopped by for one more round of cards tonight before we all head our separate ways tomorrow. Gotta go!

1. How do the camper's feelings change from Day 1 to Day 14? Use details from the text to

support your answer. _____

_____

_____

_____

_____

2. Do you think the camper will ask her Mom to attend camp again next summer, or ask to go to

her aunt's? Use details from the text to suppport your answer. _____

_____

_____

_____

_____

3. Why is it surprising that the camper's favorite activities were the zip line and ropes course?

Use details from the text to support your answer. _____

_____

_____

_____

_____

Understanding Figurative Language

Read the passage. Then, answer the questions.

Pool Day

Courtney was so excited to be going to the pool with her best friend, Elizabeth. The girls changed into their swimsuits, applied sunscreen, and grabbed their towels. Courtney had not swam since last year and was feeling a little nervous about going to the deep end. Maybe Elizabeth would just want to hang out in the kiddie pool. As soon as they arrived, Elizabeth headed straight to the diving board. Panic crept over Courtney and suddenly she felt sick as a dog. She told Elizabeth to go on and she would catch up in a minute. Courtney curled up in a lounge chair and began to cry. She watched Elizabeth swim like a fish jump after jump. Elizabeth found Courtney after a few jumps off the diving board and asked what was wrong. Courtney turned as red as a beet but decided to tell Elizabeth the truth about being scared to go in the deep end of the pool. Elizabeth hugged her and said, "Let's go to the shallow end and we'll practice swimming." Elizabeth said, "It's as easy as pie!" Courtney grinned and hugged her best friend as they walked to the shallow end of the pool.

1. "Swim like a fish" is an example of what type of figurative language? How do you know?

_____

_____

_____

2. What does "felt sick as a dog" mean in the text? Why did Courtney feel that way? Use details from the text to support your answer.

_____

_____

_____

3. In the text, Elizabeth says, "It's as easy as pie!" What is Elizabeth referring to? Use details from the text to support your answer.

_____

_____

_____

4. What does "Courtney turned as red as a beet" mean in the text? Why did she turn as red as a beet? Use details from the text to support your answer.

_____

_____

_____

Understanding Figurative Language

Read the poem. Then, answer the questions.

Thomas

I run as fast as the wind.
I am a couch potato some days though.
I eat boatloads of food every day.
I am growing faster than the weeds in my front yard.
My hair is as black as night.
My eyes are as blue as the ocean.
My heart is pure gold.

1. Line 1 of the poem uses what type of figurative language? How do you know? What does it mean?

_____

_____

2. Line 3 of the poem uses what type of figurative language? How do you know? What does it mean?

_____

_____

3. Line 7 of the poem uses what type of figurative language? How do you know? What does it mean?

_____

_____

4. What does the author mean in line 2 when he says he is a couch potato? Explain.

_____

_____

5. Write your own bio-poem and incorporate figurative language into each line. Use another sheet of paper if needed.

_____

_____

_____

_____

Point of View

Use these cards to assess students' general understanding of point of view. Assess a student quickly one-on-one by reading a card aloud and having the student give the correct point of view. Or, have students work individually or in partners to sort the cards according to point of view. If desired, laminate the cards to allow students to underline or circle the words that helped them figure out the point of view.

Lucy heard the doorbell ring and wondered who it could be. **A**	I love to go hiking in the fall. **B**
My favorite pastime is playing cards with my family. **C**	The dog ran faster and faster until he reached the open gate. **D**
Her favorite drink is pink lemonade with a cherry. **E**	The group of students made their teacher a card. **F**
I hope he gets here soon. I'm tired of waiting in the cold. **G**	I'll never forget how perfect this day has been! **H**

Understanding Point of View

Read the passage. Then, answer the questions.

Two Sides of the Same Coin

Josh and I were walking to school. Almost at the same time, we saw a bright, shiny penny on the sidewalk. Josh stepped on it.

"Aren't you gonna pick it up?" I asked.

"Yeah, right," said Josh sarcastically. "'Find a penny and pick it up, then all the day you'll have good luck.' If it were a quarter, maybe I would waste my time."

"Then, I will," I told him. "You can never have too much good luck!"

Just as we got to the school, the first bell rang. We started running to our class. One more tardy and we'd both be in trouble. As we turned the corner to our classroom, Josh wiped out and his backpack went flying. I stopped to help him pick up his stuff and scooted into the classroom as the last bell rang. Josh, who was a step or two behind me, was not so lucky. "Tardy, Josh," said Mrs. Diaz. "You will have to give me five minutes at recess."

"Please pass forward your reading assignments," Mrs. Diaz said. Josh pulled out his folder. His assignment was not there. "Are you kiddin' me? I spent three hours on it last night," he wailed.

The morning went from bad to worse. During a three-minute fact test, Josh's pencil broke. Josh only wrote two answers, and time was called. During science, his tray tipped over. Dirt, water, a plant, and science tools fell to the floor.

At lunch, I requested a piece of pepperoni pizza and got a huge slice. Josh asked for one too. "Sorry," said the cafeteria worker, "that was the last slice."

"You're sure havin' a sweet day," Josh muttered to me.

"Yeah, I guess you won't pass up any more lucky pennies," I teased.

1. From whose point of view is this passage written?

   A. Josh   B. Josh's friend   C. Mrs. Diaz   D. Josh's mom

2. What clues support your answer in question 1? Write your answer in a complete sentence.

_____

_____

3. Circle the words in the passage where the author chose to write using informal English. Why does the author use this familiar language?

_____

_____

4. Rewrite a part of the passage from another character's point of view.

_____

_____

_____

I am orange. I bounce high when filled with air. I am shot through a rim with a net. What am I?

_____

Write your own inferencing riddle.

_____

_____

A

I am warm and soft. Each stitch was made with loving hands over many hours. I keep you warm at night. What am I?

_____

Write your own inferencing riddle.

_____

_____

B

Write **3** things you liked about the story.

_____

_____

Write **2** new things you learned.

_____

_____

Write **1** question you have.

_____

C

Janelle is excited about the weekend. Her birthday party is on Saturday at the zoo!

Point of View: 1st   2nd   3rd

Rewrite the story using a different point of view.

_____

_____

D

Please don't throw the tennis ball again. I'm exhausted. Yes, my tail is wagging, but I need a break!

Point of View: 1st   2nd   3rd

Rewrite the story using a different point of view.

_____

_____

E

Match the genres to their parts.

book   stanza

drama   act

poem   chapter

Name a (book, play, poem) you like.

_____

F

Title: _____

Would you recommend this story to a friend?

Yes   No

Why or why not?

_____

_____

G

Character 1: _____

Character 2: _____

Draw a diagram to compare and contrast these two characters.

H

Setting 1: _____

Setting 2: _____
Draw a diagram to compare and contrast these two settings.

I

Genre 1: _____

Genre 2: _____
Draw a diagram to compare and contrast these two genres.

J

Determine the point of view the following would be written in.

A journal entry _____

A story about twin sisters learning to walk

_____

Rebecca's recalling of her big recital

_____

K

Title: _____

Rate your reading.

1 I couldn't read it.

2 I needed help.

3 I read most of it.

4 I read it by myself.

L

Title: _____
Color the face that shows how you feel about this text.

Explain. _____

_____

M

Max is a pig when he eats.

simile   **metaphor**

Write your own example.

_____

_____

_____

N

He has a broken heart.

simile   **metaphor**

Write your own example.

_____

_____

_____

O

Today, I'm feeling as fresh as a daisy.

simile   **metaphor**

Write your own example.

_____

_____

_____

P

Name _____ Date _____

✦ Show What You Know ✦
Reading: Informational Text

Read the passage. Then, answer the questions.

What's the Scoop?

The world has enjoyed ice-cream cones for more than 100 years. It is not entirely clear who invented the ice-cream cone, although many people believe it was the creation of Italo Marchiony, an Italian immigrant in New York City.

In the early 1900s, Marchiony owned a pushcart. He used it to sell lemon ice on the sidewalks of New York. At the time, ice cream was sold by street **vendors** in small glasses. The glasses would sometimes break or customers would walk off with them accidentally, so Marchiony decided to try something different. His first cone was made of paper. Then, he created an edible cone made from **pastry**. It became so popular that he applied for a **patent** for his edible cone.

Although Marchiony is credited with the invention of the cone, a similar creation was developed independently in 1904 at the St. Louis World's Fair. A vendor named Charles Menches had a stand there, where he sold ice cream in dishes.

One day at the fair, Menches ran out of dishes. It was very warm, and he still had several hours of business ahead of him. His friend, Ernest Hamwi, was selling a treat called *zalabia*. Zalabia was a crisp pastry sold with syrup. Menches asked his friend if he could borrow some of the zalabia. He rolled one up, scooped ice cream on top, and had an ice-cream cone.
No matter who invented the ice-cream cone, it is still popular today. One scoop, two scoops, or even three, nothing beats eating ice cream from a cone.

1. What is the main idea of the passage? Explain how you know.

_____

_____

_____

2. Based on the passage, what is a **pastry**?
- A. a vegetable
- B. a sweet baked good
- C. glue
- D. a paper cone

3. How are Marchiony and Menches similar? Use details from the text to support your answer.

_____

_____

4. How are Marchiony and Menches different? Use details from the text to support your answer.

_____

_____

5. Based on the passage, which of the following best defines the word **patent**?
   A. a smooth leather
   B. a contract to buy on loan
   C. a loose-leaf notebook
   D. a right or license to make a product

6. Which provides the best explanation for the development of Menches's cone?
   A. He was trying to help out his friend Ernest Hamwi.
   B. He knew people would love ice cream in a cone.
   C. He ran out of dishes to serve ice cream.
   D. He had sold lemon ice this way for years.

7. Why did Marchiony begin selling his ice cream out of a cone? Use details from the text to support your answer.

_____

_____

_____

_____

8. Based on the passage, what is the meaning of the word **vendor**? Use details from the text to support your answer.

_____

_____

_____

_____

✦ Show What You Know ✦
Reading: Informational Text

Read the passage. Then, answer the questions.

Ships of the Desert

Camels were once wild animals in Arabia and Asia. Long ago, they became **domesticated**. People of the desert began to use them to travel from one place to another. They also used them to **transport** objects. Camels were the perfect animals for this job because they could carry heavy loads. They can also walk and run for a long time without needing to eat or drink.

Two kinds of camels exist: the one-humped Arabian camel and the two-humped Bactrian camel. Both kinds can carry heavy loads. However, the Bactrian camel is sturdier. It can also withstand cooler climates. Arabian camels have shorter hair than Bactrian camels. Because they have only one hump, they are more likely to be trained for racing.

A camel's hump is made of fat. The animal can use it for nourishment when plants are not available on long desert walks. Camels also store water in their body tissues or in pouches inside their stomachs. The stored water help camels survive as they travel across the dry desert.

Nomadic people in North Africa and Asia still use camels. Their camels carry loads in areas without roads.

Camels are called "ships of the desert" because of their swaying motion when they walk. Among the desert dunes, they look kind of like rocking ships on a sandy sea.

1. What is the main idea of the passage? Explain how you know.

_____

_____

_____

2. Based on the passage, what is the meaning of the word **domesticated**?

    A. became extinct

    B. not useful

    C. tamed

    D. died

3. How are the Arabian camel and Bactrian camel similar? Use details from the text to support your answer.

_____

_____

_____

4. How are the Arabian camel and Bactrian camel different? Use details from the text to support your answer.

_____

_____

_____

5. Based on the passage, which of the following best defines the word **nomadic**?

    A. wandering; describes people with no fixed home

    B. rich

    C. settled; describes people with a permanent home

    D. poor

6. According to the passage, which of the following does not support why camels were used for transporting things?

    A. Camels can carry heavy loads.

    B. Camels can run extremely fast.

    C. Camels can go a long time without food.

    D. Camels can go a long time without water.

7. Describe two reasons camels are referred to as the "ships of the desert" in this passage. Use details to support your answer.

_____

_____

_____

8. Based on the passage, what is the meaning of the word **transport**? Use details from the text to explain your answer.

_____

_____

_____

Making Inferences

Read the passage. Then, make inferences from the text to answer the questions.

Save the Elephants

During the 1980s, the African elephant population declined. Originally, one million elephants existed, but this number dipped to as low as 600,000 animals. Without intervention, the African elephant would soon be an endangered species!

Thankfully, people were concerned about elephant welfare. They created organizations to protect animals, especially elephants. They devised a plan to **alleviate** the situation. They began a publicity campaign to spread awareness of the problem.

One big cause of the declining elephant population was the ivory industry. Ivory had to be harvested from elephants before being sold. Some large companies helped fix the problem by refusing to buy ivory and asking their customers to do the same.

International laws were eventually passed to make the sale of ivory illegal around the world. Once they could not sell ivory, people stopped bothering the elephants.

1. Why was the elephant population declining?

_____

2. What do you think would have happened to the African elephant if no one had made any changes? Use details from the text to support your answer.

_____

_____

3. What do you think will happen in the future now that elephants are protected? Use details from the text to support your answer.

_____

_____

4. Based on the passage, what does the word **alleviate** mean? Use details from the text to support your answer.

_____

_____

5. Why did people stop bothering the elephants? Use details from the text to support your answer.

_____

_____

Making Inferences

Read the passage. Then, make inferences from the text to answer the questions.

Vertebrates

Some scientists study animals. They classify animals by their similarities and differences. All animals can be classified into one of two groups: **vertebrates** or invertebrates. Vertebrates are animals that have backbones. Invertebrates are animals without backbones. There are five different kinds of vertebrates: amphibians, birds, fish, mammals, and reptiles. Each type of vertebrate has distinct characteristics. Some are warm-blooded, while others are cold-blooded. Body coverings, habitats, reproduction, and methods of breathing differ from one to another. The one similarity that all vertebrates share, no matter the shape or size, is a skeletal structure with a backbone.

1. Which quote from the passage best defines a **vertebrate**?

   A. Vertebrates are animals that have backbones.

   B. There are five different kinds of vertebrates: amphibians, birds, fish, mammals, and reptiles.

   C. Each type of vertebrate has distinct characteristics.

   D. All animals can be classified into one of two groups.

2. From this passage, which of the following animals can you infer are vertebrates? Circle all of the answers that apply.

   A. butterfly

   B. dog

   C. dolphin

   D. jellyfish

3. Based on the information from the passage, list three more animals that are vertebrates.

   _____

   _____

   _____

4. Based on the information from the passage, list the characteristics that may differ from one kind of invertebrate to another.

   _____

   _____

Determining Main Idea

Read each group of sentences and phrases. Write **T** for topic (1), **MI** for main idea (1), and **SD** for supporting details (2).

1. _____ They are light and fluffy, and they melt in your mouth.

_____ Scrambled eggs

_____ Scrambled eggs are a delicious breakfast item.

_____ They are especially tasty mixed with cheese and bacon bits.

2. _____ The gamma-ray spectrometer is an amazing invention.

_____ It is a highly sensitive instrument used to map elements on the moon.

_____ Gamma-ray spectrometer

_____ It maps the elements on the moon by recording gamma rays and neutrons.

3. _____ Velcro

_____ It enables children to put on their own shoes before they know how to tie laces.

_____ It helps attach many clothing items and is an alternative to zippers and buttons.

_____ Velcro is a useful invention.

4. _____ Pet owners are happier and healthier than non–pet owners.

_____ Pet ownership

_____ Owners' anxiety levels decrease as they interact with their pet.

_____ It is fun to pet and play with animals.

5. _____ The Goliath birdeater can weigh up to 170 grams.

_____ Spiders come in all shapes and sizes.

_____ The male patu digua is only as large as the head of a pin.

_____ Spiders

Name _____   Date _____

Determining Main Idea

Read the passage. Think about the topic, main idea, and supporting details. Then, complete the graphic organizer.

Infectious Disease

Viral infectious diseases can be as frightening today as they were in the past when they meant almost certain death. Viral diseases are contagious. They can become a health hazard.

An epidemic is an infectious disease that affects a large number of people. In an epidemic, the infection spreads quickly and lasts a long time. The plague, or Black Death, is an example of an epidemic. It spread through fleas that were infected by black rats.

A pandemic is even more widespread than an epidemic. A pandemic is an infectious disease that spreads across the world. Smallpox is an example of a pandemic.

An endemic is an infectious disease that continues in certain areas or populations all of the time. It is often caused by an abnormality in plant or animal life in that area. Malaria is one example of an endemic. It is transported by mosquitoes.

Over time, immunizations and medications have been invented to help fight some of these diseases and treat their symptoms. But, for many, there is still no cure.

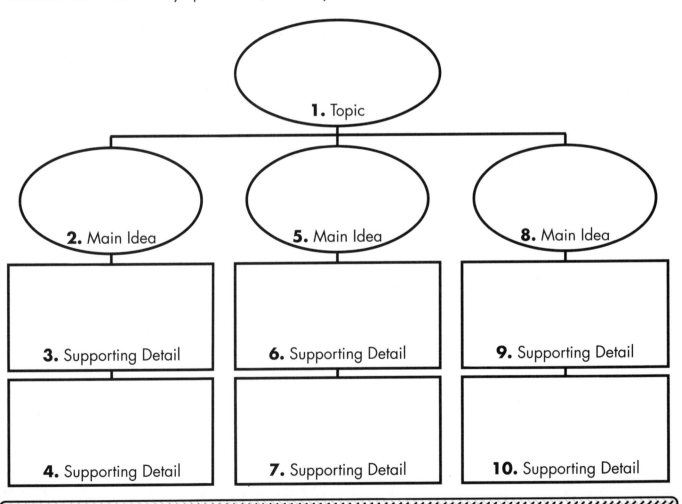

Determining Main Idea

Read the passage. Then, answer the questions.

Moon Phases

Why does the moon look different on different nights? Does it really change shape? No; as the moon rotates around Earth, the moon is **illuminated** by light from the sun. We see the different fractions of the moon that is lit by the sun. These are known as the phases of the moon. Here on Earth, we watch the moon change from a thin crescent to a full moon and back to a thin crescent. It takes about 29.5 days for our moon to cycle through all phases. There are eight major phases. The phases are named after how much of the moon we can see and whether the part we can see is getting bigger or smaller.

1. What is the main idea of the passage?

A. The moon orbits the Earth.

B. It takes about 29.5 days for our moon to cycle through all phases.

C. The phases of the moon are caused by the part of the moon that is lit by the sun.

D. The moon changes shape each month.

2. Based on the passage, what does **illuminated** mean?

_____

3. Topic: _____

Main Idea: _____

Supporting Detail: _____

Supporting Detail: _____

4. According to the text, why does the moon appear different each night?

A. The moon changes shapes as it orbits Earth.

B. The shadow from the moon causes the different phases.

C. The shadow from the sun causes the different phases.

D. Different amounts of the moon are lit by light from the sun as it orbits Earth.

5. Reread the passage and write a summary.

_____

_____

_____

Comparing and Contrasting

Read the passage. Look for relationships between the explorers in the text. Then, answer the questions.

English Explorers

The Age of Exploration began in the 1400s. Many Europeans looked to the ocean and wondered what lay across the horizon. England produced many such explorers.

One of the earliest English explorers of North America was John Cabot, who set sail in 1497. Cabot was looking for a new route from England to Asia, but instead he found the eastern coast of what is now Canada. He explored places currently known as Newfoundland, Labrador, and Nova Scotia.

Another explorer, Sir Francis Drake, sailed from England in the 1580s. He was the first Englishman to **circumnavigate**, or sail all the way around, the world.

Henry Hudson sailed from England to the New World in the early 1600s. He was looking for a passageway across North America by water from the Atlantic Ocean to the Pacific Ocean. He did not find this passageway; however, his discoveries did result in the body of water known as the Hudson Bay that is named for him.

1. What did the men in this passage have in common?

    A. They are all explorers from England.

    B. They were explorers who sailed together to the New World.

    C. They were the first explorers to discover North America.

    D. They were all explorers from the 1500s.

2. Name two things Cabot, Drake, and Hudson had in common.

_____

_____

3. Name one way that two of the men were different. Write your answer in a complete sentence.

_____

4. Based on the passage, what does the word **circumnavigate** mean?

_____

_____

5. Explain what "The Age of Exploration" is using details from the text to support your answer.

_____

_____

Name _____ Date _____

Comparing and Contrasting

Read the passage. Then, answer the questions.

Dynamic Duo

Remember reading about the abolitionists of the American Civil War? They wanted to see slaves freed. They wanted slaves to have equal rights. Elizabeth Cady Stanton was an abolitionist. Stanton came to a World Anti-Slavery Convention in London. When she arrived, she became angry when she discovered women were not able to speak or vote at the convention.

At the convention, Stanton met other women who were also unhappy because women were not recognized at the meetings. The women planned special meetings to talk about these problems. They called their own convention to improve women's rights. The convention was held in Seneca Falls, New York. It helped launch a movement toward equal rights for women. This movement was first called "woman suffrage." It sought to extend women's rights to vote, run for office, and receive fair wages.

Meanwhile, Susan B. Anthony was working to convince industries to hire and pay women equal to men. She fought for the right of women to join trade unions run by men. Stanton soon developed a working relationship with Anthony. The two made a great team. Stanton wanted to help women, but she did not want to travel. She had young children at home. Stanton was writing speeches for Anthony to deliver across the country. Anthony was single and had no children.

The pair founded the National Woman Suffrage Association. Stanton became its president. Anthony was always the more popular and better known of the two. Her travel back and forth across the country made her familiar to many Americans. She devoted all of her efforts to women's rights to vote and hold office. She is best remembered for this. Stanton was involved in many areas of reform for women. She did not think that voting was any more important than the right to hold political office or own property. Elizabeth Cady Stanton's husband once told her, "You stir up Susan, and Susan stirs up the world!"

1. Which best describes the relationship between Stanton and Anthony?

A. Stanton and Anthony were best friends since childhood.

B. Stanton and Anthony worked together to improve women's rights.

C. Stanton and Anthony were sisters.

D. Stanton and Anthony worked together to abolish slavery.

2. Stanton was fighting against _____ when she discovered _____ were not able to speak or vote at the convention. Stanton's focus then shifted to improving women's _____.

3. Use the Venn diagram to compare and contrast the two women.

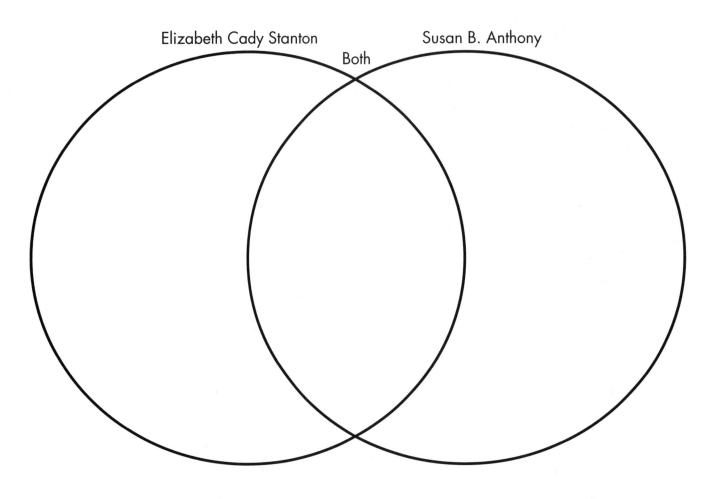

Elizabeth Cady Stanton   Both   Susan B. Anthony

4. Write a short summary of the passage.

_____

_____

_____

_____

_____

_____

_____

_____

Understanding Text Structure

Read the table of contents. Then, answer the questions.

1. Based on the information in the table of contents, what is an **arachnid**?

A. a spider

B. an insect

C. a type of creature such as a spider or a scorpion

D. a vegetable

2. On what page or pages could you read specific information about spiders? Circle the best answer.

A. pages 1–16   B. page 14

C. page 16   D. pages 19–20

3. Based on the information in the table of contents, what type of book is this?

A. a scientific book written for scientists who study arachnids

B. a science book written for children about arachnids

C. a fictional story about arachnids

D. a biography

4. What information from the table of contents helped you answer question 3?

_____

_____

5. Would you enjoy reading this book? Why or why not?

_____

Name _____ Date _____

Understanding Text Structure

Read the table of contents. Then, answer the questions.

Table of Contents	
The Atmosphere	4
The Ozone Layer	6
How Much Ozone?	8
Chlorofluorocarbons and Ozone	10
Destroying Ozone	12
The Effects of Humans	18
What Can Be Done	20
Glossary	24

1. Based on the information in the table of contents, what would be a good title for this book?

_____

2. On what page or pages could you find the definition of **chlorofluorocarbons**?

   A. page 10

   B. page 24

   C. pages 10, 11, and 24

   D. pages 12–17

3. Based on the information in the table of contents, what type of book is this?

   A. a scientific book written for scientists who study the ozone

   B. a science fiction story about living in the ozone layer

   C. a science book written for anyone about the ozone

   D. a scientific book about the planets

4. What information from the table of contents helped you answer question 3?

_____

_____

5. Would you enjoy reading this book? Why or why not?

_____

_____

_____

Understanding Text Structure

Read the recipe. Then, answer the questions.

Grilled Cheese Sandwich
Makes 1 serving

Ingredients:
butter or margarine
2 slices of bread
1 slice of cheese
1 slice of ham (**optional**)

Directions:
Place **skillet** on burner on medium heat. Butter two slices of bread. Stack buttered sides together on a plate. Add cheese (and ham, if desired) to the top slice of bread. Place top slice of bread with cheese (and ham) in skillet, buttered side down. Top with other slice, buttered side up. Toast until golden brown and cheese starts to melt. Flip and toast other side. When toasted evenly, remove from heat. Cut in half and serve on a plate.

1. What is this a recipe for? _____

2. How are the ingredients organized?
    A. alphabetically
    B. from largest amount to smallest amount
    C. in the order the ingredients are used
    D. numerically

3. Based on the text, what does the word **optional** mean?
    A. recommended   B. not necessary, but a choice
    C. unnecessary and not recommended   D. mandatory

4. In the recipe, what does the word **skillet** mean? How do you know? _____

_____

_____

5. What is the main purpose of this selection?
    A. to tell people how to make breakfast
    B. to tell a story about how something was invented
    C. to tell people how to do something
    D. to persuade people to have a picnic

Name _____ Date _____

Understanding Point of View

Read the passage. Then, answer the questions.

Volcanoes

There are many kinds of volcanoes. Each kind of volcano erupts differently. A composite volcano has violent eruptions. Mount St. Helens is a composite volcano. Mount St. Helens is in the state of Washington. It erupted in 1980. Almost all of the trees within miles were killed by the blast. Geologists predicted it with scientific tools. Few people were killed or injured due to the early warning. Mount Vesuvius in Italy is a composite volcano too. It erupted in the year 79. The lava and ash from the eruption completely covered a nearby town. The people near the volcano had no warning, because it happened very quickly. Archaeologists **excavating** the city found it frozen in place in the middle of a normal day.

1. Which eruption affected a larger number of people? Use details from the passage to show how you know.

_____

_____

2. What is the biggest similarity between the two eruptions?

_____

_____

3. What is the biggest difference between the two eruptions?

_____

4. Based on the passage, what does the word **excavating** mean?
   A. destroying
   B. trying to save or defend
   C. trying to reuse or recycle
   D. digging out or uncovering

5. What is the author's point of view? Use details from the text to support your answer.

_____

_____

6. Does the author think geology and scientific tools are helpful? Explain.

_____

_____

Understanding Point of View

Read the two journal entries. Then, answer the questions.

Farm Life

Farmer Joe

    Farm life is amazing. I just love waking up with the roosters each and every morning. I love that peaceful moment in time when the world isn't awake yet and the sun hasn't even fully shown itself. In the still of the morning, I look around and am thankful for this farm. After drinking my coffee while watching the sunrise each morning, I prepare for my invigorating day.

    First, I tend to all of the animals. We have chickens, cows, pigs, and horses. I'm not sure who's happier to see whom. It is such a joy interacting with them each morning. After the animals, I head to the barn for Ol' Red. Most of my days during harvest season are spent on my tractor. Long days of nothing but the fields, Ol' Red, and me. Row after row, we reap what we've sown. As soon as Ol' Red is parked for the day, I spend another hour or so mending fences, cleaning up, and checking on the animals.

    What a beautiful day. I look forward to another day of farm life tomorrow.

Farmer Jeff

    Why can't the roosters sleep past 6 am? Every single morning, I dread this natural alarm clock. I wish they would at least wait until the sun is completely up before they start. I might as well get up and get started on my day.

    First, I better check on the animals. I have never in my life seen such messy animals. The pigs have torn up their trough again. I guess I'll need to fix that too. Finally, I finish up and can get out to the fields. An entire day spent on nothing but sitting and harvesting. I didn't think the day would ever end.

    I should get to sleep because I have to get up and do it all over again in the morning.

1. Both farmers are writing about what topic?

_____

2. How does Farmer Joe feel about the topic? Use specific details from the text to support your answer.

_____

_____

_____

3. How does Farmer Jeff feel about the topic? Use specific details from the text to support your answer.

_____

_____

_____

4. Complete the Venn diagram below based on the two journal entries.

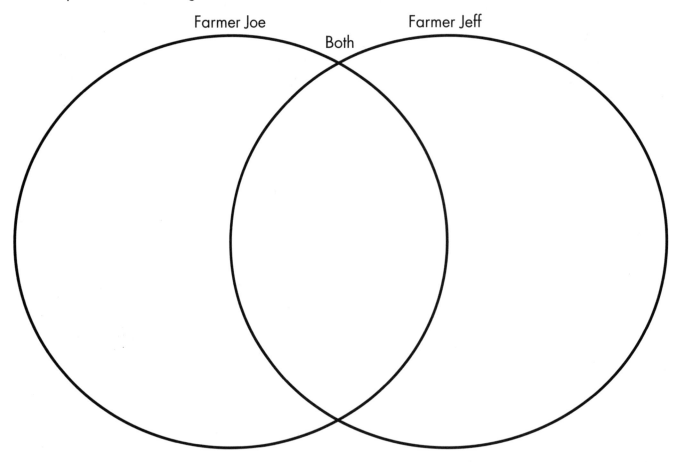

Farmer Joe   Both   Farmer Jeff

Topic of Text: _____

Main Idea of Text: _____

Supporting Details: _____

_____

_____

_____

A

This text is arranged _____ .

    A. chronologically

    B. by problem/solution

    C. by cause/effect

    D. by comparison/contrast

I know this because _____

_____ .

B

Compare and contrast a firsthand and secondhand account of the same topic.

Topic: _____

C

Choose two points from a text to show how the author used reasoning in an effective way.

Point made by author: _____

_____

Evidence to support point: _____

_____

_____

D

Rate your reading.

    1 I couldn't read it.

    2 I needed help.

    3 I read most of it.

    4 I read it by myself.

E

Title: _____

Color the face that shows how you feel about this text.

Explain. _____

_____

F

Provide information from two texts on the same topic.

Title: _____   Title: _____

Information: _____   Information: _____

_____ _____

_____ _____

_____ _____

G

Unfamiliar word: _____

Text clues I used to help me understand the word:

_____

_____

_____

_____

H

The two people that I read about were
_____ and _____. Using
a Venn diagram, compare and contrast these
two people.

I

The two events that I read about were
_____ and _____. Using
a Venn diagram, compare and contrast these
two events.

J

The two ideas that I read about were
_____ and _____. Using
a Venn diagram, compare and contrast these
two ideas.

K

How can you combine information from
both texts to support your thinking about this
topic?

_____

_____

_____

_____

_____

L

Summarize the topic you read about. Write in
complete sentences.

_____

_____

_____

_____

_____

M

List three things that good readers do.

• _____

• _____

• _____

N

Title _____

Would you recommend this text to a friend?

Yes   **No**

Why or why not?

_____

_____

O

Describe the inference you were able to make
while reading the text. Use details from the
text to support your inference.

_____

_____

_____

_____

_____

P

The Dilemma

The little ant lugged the sandwich crumb through one tunnel after another. It was such a relief to be out of the blazing sunlight. Even though he was tired and **weary**, he kept going. He knew the need for food was important, but still, the fable of the grasshopper and the ant bothered him. Of course, they needed food to eat and a safe, warm home, but wasn't fun necessary too?

That night after much pondering, the little ant talked to his wise grandmother about his question. "Grandmother, all I do is work. Every day is the same old thing: find a crumb, and bring it to the anthill. Why can't I enjoy life just a little?"

"You can't fill your belly with fun," Grandmother replied.

The little ant felt sad and a bit depressed. "Surely there must be a way to have fun and still work hard," he thought to himself. "Maybe if I just spent a little time having fun, then I could grab an extra crumb and still do my part. Besides, wouldn't I be more productive after a little rest or a bit of fun?"

The next day, the little ant followed the other ants towards the opening of the anthill. But, when he reached the top, a smile spread across his face. There were plenty of detours and fun to be had between the anthill and that picnic. Today would be an unforgettable adventure, the little ant determined.

What an exciting day the little ant had. His adventure energized him. After a bit, the little ant scurried to the picnic and loaded up with an extra crumb or two. Then, he quickly joined his fellow ants on their trek back to the anthill. Yes, fun could add to his productivity and the quality of his life!

The Dilemma

The little ant lugged the sandwich crumb through one tunnel after another. It was	14

The little ant lugged the sandwich crumb through one tunnel after another. It was   14
such a relief to be out of the blazing sunlight. Even though he was tired and **weary**,   31
he kept going. He knew the need for food was important, but still, the fable of the   48
grasshopper and the ant bothered him. Of course, they needed food to eat and a safe,   64
warm home, but wasn't fun necessary too?   71

That night after much pondering, the little ant talked to his wise grandmother   84
about his question. "Grandmother, all I do is work. Every day is the same old thing: find   101
a crumb, and bring it to the anthill. Why can't I enjoy life just a little?"   117

"You can't fill your belly with fun," Grandmother replied.   126

The little ant felt sad and a bit depressed. "Surely there must be a way to have   143
fun and still work hard," he thought to himself. "Maybe if I just spent a little time having   161
fun, then I could grab an extra crumb and still do my part. Besides, wouldn't I be more   179
productive after a little rest or a bit of fun?"   189

The next day, the little ant followed the other ants towards the opening of the   204
anthill. But, when he reached the top, a smile spread across his face. There were plenty   220
of detours and fun to be had between the anthill and that picnic. Today would be an   237
unforgettable adventure, the little ant determined.   243

What an exciting day the little ant had. His adventure energized him. After a bit,   259
the little ant scurried to the picnic and loaded up with an extra crumb or two. Then, he   276
quickly joined his fellow ants on their trek back to the anthill. Yes, fun could add to his   294
productivity and the quality of his life!   301

Number of Words Read	Words per Minute	Words Read in Error
First Try		
Second Try		
Third Try		

The Water Park

"Twenty-five, fifty, seventy-five, eighty, eighty-one, eighty-two . . . that's $47.82," counted Carter. He gathered the change and placed it next to the bills on the red comforter. Then, he flopped back onto the bed, making the change bounce.

"**Rats**! We still need $16.18 to cover the admission cost," pouted Kevin. "Mom said we have to have the total cost of admission before we can go to Super Soaker Park."

The two boys lay on the beds in their room, imagining the theme park: tasty treats like ice-cream bars, shaved ice, and frozen drinks; enormous slides that wound around like a corkscrew; and endless pools of varying depths. It even had a winding river where you could float on inner tubes. Now that was the way to beat the heat!

"We won't have enough for two more weeks with our allowances," said Carter.

"I know," Kevin agreed, "and I've already checked between the couch cushions, under the car seats, and in all of our jacket pockets."

The two sat contemplating the situation. Suddenly, at the exact same time, an idea popped into their heads.

"Let's ask Mom if we can do some extra chores around the house to earn more money," suggested Kevin. Carter nodded as Kevin spoke.

Sure enough, their mom was more than happy to pay the boys to do some extra chores around the house. She had wanted the garage cleaned for a while but couldn't find the time. The boys worked hard and grumbled a bit as they did. But, when the garage was clean, their mom was pleased with their work and paid them $10.00 each. That, together with what they already had, was enough for admission to the water park!

The Water Park

"Twenty-five, fifty, seventy-five, eighty, eighty-one, eighty-two . . . that's $47.82,"   12
counted Carter. He gathered the change and placed it next to the bills on the red   29
comforter. Then, he flopped back onto the bed, making the change bounce.   36

"**Rats**! We still need $16.18 to cover the admission cost," pouted Kevin. "Mom   49
said we have to have the total cost of admission before we can go to Super Soaker Park."   67

The two boys lay on the beds in their room, imagining the theme park: tasty treats   83
like ice-cream bars, shaved ice, and frozen drinks; enormous slides that wound around   97
like a corkscrew; and endless pools of varying depths. It even had a winding river where   113
you could float on inner tubes. Now that was the way to beat the heat!   128

"We won't have enough for two more weeks with our allowances," said Carter.   141

"I know," Kevin agreed, "and I've already checked between the couch cushions,   153
under the car seats, and in all of our jacket pockets."   164

The two sat contemplating the situation. Suddenly, at the exact same time, an idea   178
popped into their heads.   182

"Let's ask Mom if we can do some extra chores around the house to earn more   198
money," suggested Kevin. Carter nodded as Kevin spoke.   206

Sure enough, their mom was more than happy to pay the boys to do some extra   222
chores around the house. She had wanted the garage cleaned for a while but couldn't   237
find the time. The boys worked hard and grumbled a bit as they did. But, when the   254
garage was clean, their mom was pleased with their work and paid them $10.00 each.   269
That, together with what they already had, was enough for admission to the water park!   284

Number of Words Read	Words per Minute	Words Read in Error
First Try		
Second Try		
Third Try		

Light Show in the Sky

It was dark. The sky was deep blue with pinpoint stars winking in the distance. The nearly leafless trees stretched their trembling arms towards the sky. Megan and Madison shivered in their lawn chairs as they pulled the stadium blanket they shared more tightly around themselves. They were full of **anticipation**.

The conditions were just right. The newscaster had announced the solar winds traveling towards the earth. It was certain to happen tonight.

Orion's belt rose slowly in the southeastern sky. The Big Dipper hovered, waiting for a scoop of color. A slight shimmer started in the west, a hint of faded blue teasing the eyes. Slowly the colors intensified. Greens flowed through the sky from the north like vines of ivy, reaching south and rolling in waves from east to west and back again.

Then, the vines turned red like party streamers, contrasting vividly with the velvet blue sky. The aurora borealis, or northern lights, shimmered spectacularly across the sky. The vivid colors danced through the darkness with such elegance. Then, they dimmed, faded, and disappeared just as quickly as they had appeared.

The girls sat speechless, hoping for an encore, but slowly the cold seeped into the awe. Shivering, they gathered their blankets and chairs and walked silently back into the house. It was a scene they wouldn't soon forget.

Light Show in the Sky

It was dark. The sky was deep blue with pinpoint stars winking in the distance. The   16
nearly leafless trees stretched their trembling arms towards the sky. Megan and Madison   29
shivered in their lawn chairs as they pulled the stadium blanket they shared more tightly   44
around themselves. They were full of **anticipation**.   51

The conditions were just right. The newscaster had announced the solar winds   63
traveling towards the earth. It was certain to happen tonight.   73

Orion's belt rose slowly in the southeastern sky. The Big Dipper hovered, waiting   86
for a scoop of color. A slight shimmer started in the west, a hint of faded blue teasing the   105
eyes. Slowly the colors intensified. Greens flowed through the sky from the north like vines   120
of ivy, reaching south and rolling in waves from east to west and back again.   135

Then, the vines turned red like party streamers, contrasting vividly with the velvet   148
blue sky. The aurora borealis, or northern lights, shimmered spectacularly across the sky.   161
The vivid colors danced through the darkness with such elegance. Then, they dimmed,   174
faded, and disappeared just as quickly as they had appeared.   184

The girls sat speechless, hoping for an encore, but slowly the cold seeped into the   199
awe. Shivering, they gathered their blankets and chairs and walked silently back into the   213
house. It was a scene they wouldn't soon forget.   222

Number of Words Read	Words per Minute	Words Read in Error
First Try		
Second Try		
Third Try		

Name _____ Date _____

Whales

Whales are mammals that live in water. Most whales live in the ocean, but there are some that live in freshwater rivers. Whales vary in size, but most are quite large. In fact, the blue whale is the biggest creature to have ever lived on Earth!

Because whales are mammals, they have lungs and breathe air. They have openings on the tops of their heads called blowholes. Whales come to the surface to breathe. The blowhole opens each time the whale surfaces, causing water to spray up. The blowhole closes before the whale dives back under the water.

Most whales fall into one of two categories of whales. There are toothed whales and baleen whales. Toothed whales have teeth and baleen whales do not. Instead, baleen whales have **baleen**. Baleen acts like a strainer, filtering small fish and plankton out of the water so that the whale can eat them.

Whales have a thick layer of fat called blubber. Blubber keeps the whale buoyant in the water, preventing it from sinking. Blubber insulates the whale, helping it to maintain its body temperature in cold waters. Whales can also use the blubber as an energy source when food is scarce.

Whales were hunted close to extinction years ago. They were hunted mostly for their blubber. The blubber was used for lamp oil, cosmetics, soap, and various other things. Whales are no longer hunted as much, but pollution now endangers their existence. Several groups are working hard to protect the whales. Because of this, whales are increasing in number, but it will take many, many years to increase the population back to where they are no longer endangered.

Whales

Whales are mammals that live in water. Most whales live in the ocean, but there   15
are some that live in freshwater rivers. Whales vary in size, but most are quite large. In   32
fact, the blue whale is the biggest creature to have ever lived on Earth!   46

Because whales are mammals, they have lungs and breathe air. They have   58
openings on the tops of their heads called blowholes. Whales come to the surface to   73
breathe. The blowhole opens each time the whale surfaces, causing water to spray up.   87
The blowhole closes before the whale dives back under the water.   98

Most whales fall into one of two categories of whales. There are toothed whales   112
and baleen whales. Toothed whales have teeth and baleen whales do not. Instead,   125
baleen whales have **baleen**. Baleen acts like a strainer, filtering small fish and plankton   139
out of the water so that the whale can eat them.   150

Whales have a thick layer of fat called blubber. Blubber keeps the whale buoyant   164
in the water, preventing it from sinking. Blubber insulates the whale, helping it to maintain   179
its body temperature in cold waters. Whales can also use the blubber as an energy   194
source when food is scarce.   199

Whales were hunted close to extinction years ago. They were hunted mostly   211
for their blubber. The blubber was used for lamp oil, cosmetics, soap and various   225
other things. Whales are no longer hunted as much, but pollution now endangers their   239
existence. Several groups are working hard to protect the whales. Because of this, whales   253
are increasing in number, but it will take many, many years to increase the population   268
back to where they are no longer endangered.   276

Number of Words Read	Words per Minute	Words Read in Error
First Try		
Second Try		
Third Try		

The Truth about History

History is not always what it seems. Imagine that your favorite basketball team is the Houston Rockets. You missed an unbelievable game they played against the Los Angeles Lakers. You know that the Rockets won, but you want to find out more. You want to know how they won. When you ask your friends about the game, they each tell you something different.

For example, during overtime, the referees called a **controversial** foul. One of your friends says, "The Lakers would have won if it weren't for that call." Another friend argues that the foul was a good call. Both sides mix facts with their opinions about what they saw.

You decide to check the newspapers for the real story. At home, you look at newspapers online from both Houston, Texas, and Los Angeles, California. The stories from these two newspapers disagree. Both sides sound good, but both sides did not tell the whole truth.

Next, you decide to watch a video of the game. Even the instant replay is not very clear.

It is difficult to get to the truth about something that you did not witness. Imagine a game that was played 100 years ago. You would have to rely on written accounts, such as newspaper articles from that time or a diary kept by one of the players. Historians look at evidence like this to help recreate historic events. But, many events are much more complicated than the outcome of a basketball game. Think about how many different opinions there are about the American Revolution.

History can be defined as a "best guess." When we try to look at history, it is almost as if we are detectives trying to piece together clues. We have to decide what happened based on the evidence left behind. We cannot know for sure, because we were not there.

History is not always what it seems. Imagine that your favorite basketball team   13
is the Houston Rockets. You missed an unbelievable game they played against the Los   27
Angeles Lakers. You know that the Rockets won, but you want to find out more. You want   44
to know how they won. When you ask your friends about the game, they each tell you   61
something different.   63

For example, during overtime, the referees called a **controversial** foul. One of   75
your friends says, "The Lakers would have won if it weren't for that call." Another friend   91
argues that the foul was a good call. Both sides mix facts with their opinions about what   108
they saw.   110

You decide to check the newspapers for the real story. At home, you look at   125
newspapers online from both Houston, Texas, and Los Angeles, California. The stories   137
from these two newspapers disagree. Both sides sound good, but both sides did not tell   152
the whole truth.   155

Next, you decide to watch a video of the game. Even the instant replay is not   171
very clear.   173

It is difficult to get to the truth about something that you did not witness. Imagine a   190
game that was played 100 years ago. You would have to rely on written accounts, such   206
as newspaper articles from that time or a diary kept by one of the players. Historians   222
look at evidence like this to help recreate historic events. But, many events are much more   238
complicated than the outcome of a basketball game. Think about how many different   251
opinions there are about the American Revolution.   258

History can be defined as a "best guess." When we try to look at history, it is   275
almost as if we are detectives trying to piece together clues. We have to decide what   291
happened based on the evidence left behind. We cannot know for sure, because we   305
were not there.   308

Number of Words Read	Words per Minute	Words Read in Error
First Try		
Second Try		
Third Try		

Blink of an Eye

    Blinking is the opening and closing of the eyelid. The average person blinks once every four seconds. That is about 15 times per minute during the waking hours of every day. So when you think about it, the average person blinks about 15,000 times each day!

    Eyelids are folds of skin that are raised and lowered by muscles. The lids of our eyes move much like the windshield wipers in a car. However, they move very quickly, so our vision is not **impaired**. Why do we blink, and why is blinking so important?

    For one thing, blinking helps protect our eyes. Most of the eye is enclosed in a bony socket covered with a protective layer of fat. But, part of the surface area becomes exposed when the eyes open. Eyelashes help keep dust and other small particles out. However, sometimes they still get into the eye. Blinking helps remove irritants to keep the eyes from becoming damaged. If you start blinking fiercely, it probably means you have something in your eye. Blinking also keeps the eyes **lubricated**. Along the edge of each eyelid are several tiny tear glands. They are located in between eyelashes. Every time an eyelid blinks, the glands release fluid. A film of tears coats the eye and prevents it from becoming too dry.

    Have you ever had your picture taken and your eyes started to blink rapidly? That is because blinking also protects eyes from bright lights. You may also blink more when cutting fresh onions. The onions release a gas that makes the eyes tear up and blink. Getting smoke in your eyes can make you blink more too.

    There are also emotional reasons for why we blink. Our eyes tend to blink more during times of anxiety or stress than when we are calm. We tend to blink less when we are busy concentrating. Fatigue, disease, and injury to the eye can also affect how often we blink.

Blink of an Eye

Blinking is the opening and closing of the eyelid. The average person blinks once 14
every four seconds. That is about 15 times per minute during the waking hours of every 30
day. So when you think about it, the average person blinks about 15,000 times 44
each day! 46

Eyelids are folds of skin that are raised and lowered by muscles. The lids of our 62
eyes move much like the windshield wipers in a car. However, they move very quickly, so 78
our vision is not **impaired**. Why do we blink, and why is blinking so important? 93

For one thing, blinking helps protect our eyes. Most of the eye is enclosed in a 109
bony socket covered with a protective layer of fat. But, part of the surface area becomes 125
exposed when the eyes open. Eyelashes help keep dust and other small particles out. 139
However, sometimes they still get into the eye. Blinking helps remove irritants to keep the 154
eyes from becoming damaged. If you start blinking fiercely, it probably means you have 168
something in your eye. Blinking also keeps the eyes **lubricated**. Along the edge of each 183
eyelid are several tiny tear glands. They are located in between eyelashes. Every time an 198
eyelid blinks, the glands release fluid. A film of tears coats the eye and prevents it from 215
becoming too dry. 218

Have you ever had your picture taken and your eyes started to blink rapidly? That 233
is because blinking also protects eyes from bright lights. You may also blink more when 248
cutting fresh onions. The onions release a gas that makes the eyes tear up and blink. 264
Getting smoke in your eyes can make you blink more too. 275

There are also emotional reasons for why we blink. Our eyes tend to blink more 290
during times of anxiety or stress than when we are calm. We tend to blink less when we 308
are busy concentrating. Fatigue, disease, and injury to the eye can also affect how often 323
we blink. 325

Number of Words Read	Words per Minute	Words Read in Error
First Try		
Second Try		
Third Try		

Fluency Comprehension Questions

The Dilemma (pages 49 and 50)
1. What is the meaning of **weary** in the text?
2. What is the moral of the fable?
3. Explain why a smile spread across his face.
4. What point of view is the story told from?

The Water Park (pages 51 and 52)
1. What is the meaning of **rats** in the passage?
2. What is the problem in the story?
3. What is the solution in the story?
4. Where is the setting?

Light Show in the Sky (pages 53 and 54)
1. What is the meaning of **anticipation** in the passage?
2. Where were the girls?
3. What were the girls doing?
4. Why do you think it is a night they wouldn't soon forget?

Whales (pages 55 and 56)
1. Why do whales have openings on the tops of their heads?
2. Why do whales have blubber? Give at least two reasons.
3. What is **baleen**?
4. Why were whales hunted?

The Truth About History (pages 57 and 58)
1. Why were the newspaper accounts different from one another?
2. Why is it hard to know whether history is accurate?
3. What is the meaning of **controversial** in the text?
4. What is another possible title for this passage?

Blink of an Eye (pages 59 and 60)
1. What is the meaning of **impaired** in the text?
2. Why do we blink? Give at least 2 reasons.
3. What is the meaning of **lubricated** in the text?
4. How often does the average person blink?

Word Lists

Use these lists of words when you are assessing language concepts. The lists are not comprehensive but can be used as grade-level examples for creating your own assessments, flash cards, etc.

Prefixes
disappear
discontinue
impassable
impossible
inaccurate
international
interrupt
intramural
intravenous
invisible
microphone
microscope
misbehave
misfortune
nonresistant
nonsense
precaution
prepare
reappear
rewrite
submarine
submerge
telephone
telescope
transatlantic
transport
uncertain
uncomfortable

Suffixes
actor
agreeable
beggar
careless
childish
citizenship
development
driver
editor
enjoyable
erosion
experiment
forgetful
friendship
happily
harmless
kindness
liar
lighten
lonely
luckiest
performer
pollution
selfish
sickness
softest
strengthen
successful

Roots
activity
admit
aquarium
aquatic
autobiography
bankrupt
biology
chronological
conform
contradict
dictate
disruption
eject
formation
inscription
inspection
interject
perimeter
photograph
photosynthesis
portable
prescribe
react
spectator
synchronize
thermometer
transmit
transportation

Word Lists

Irregular Plural Nouns
children
deer
echoes
geese
halves
heroes
loaves
men
people
sheep
shelves
teeth
wolves
women

Abstract Nouns
anger
childhood
compassion
courage
faith
friendship
justice
love
loyalty
peace
pride
reality
trust
wisdom

Irregular Verbs
begin/began/begun
break/broke/broken
choose/chose/chosen
draw/drew/drawn
drive/drove/driven
fly/flew/flown
give/gave/given
know/knew/known
ride/rode/ridden
ring/rang/rung
show/showed/shown
swim/swam/swum
take/took/taken
wake/woke/woken

Homographs
bass
close
conduct
fair
lead
match
minute
object
park
perfect
present
produce
tear
yard

Spelling Patterns
announce
blizzard
chore
employ
knuckle
loyal
moisture
paragraph
poison
pour
powder
stern
third
voyage

Multi-Syllabic Words
antibiotics
autobiography
catastrophe
committee
emergency
encyclopedia
foundation
livelihood
occupation
perpendicular
precipitation
quadrilateral
unimaginable
unsatisfactory

A

List three words you had trouble decoding today. List the strategy that helped you.

B

Find three words from your text with an affix. Complete the chart below.

Prefix	Base	Suffix

C

Correct each irregularly spelled word. Then, write a sentence using each.

shelfs _____

_____

trophys _____

_____

wierd _____

_____

D

Match the following affixes to their meanings. Then, write a sentence using at least two of the affixes.

pre-   without
-less   not, opposite of
un-   again
re-   before

_____

_____

E

Write two sentences for each homograph.

lead _____

_____

_____

fair _____

_____

_____

F

Choose the correct verb tense for the following sentences.

She (give/gave/given) him a book yesterday during class.

How long have you (know/knew/known) him?

I plan to (swim/swam/swum) all afternoon.

G

Turn to page _____ in your _____ book.

List all of the words you find containing prefixes and/or suffixes. Then, list the meaning of each affix.

H

Today, I read _____ words per minute.

At this point, I should be reading _____ words per minute.

My goal is to read _____ words per minute on my next timed reading.

Opinion Writing Prompts

Use these cards to assess students' ability to write opinion pieces on topics or texts, supporting a point of view with reasons and information. Use one card for a whole-class assessment, or place the cards in a writing center and allow students to choose a prompt to write about.

Which kind of pet is best, a dog or a cat? **A**	Should schools assign nightly homework? **B**
Should students be required to wear school uniforms? **C**	Should children ages 10 and under have their own cell phone? **D**
Write about your favorite subject. Why is it your favorite? Do you think everyone should be required to study this subject? **E**	Should school be year-round? **F**
Write a letter to your principal explaining why recess should be longer. **G**	Which holiday do you believe is the best? **H**

Informative/Explanatory Writing Prompts

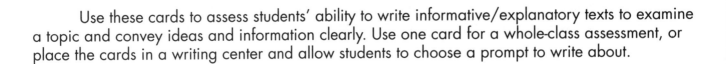

Use these cards to assess students' ability to write informative/explanatory texts to examine a topic and convey ideas and information clearly. Use one card for a whole-class assessment, or place the cards in a writing center and allow students to choose a prompt to write about.

Write a short biography about your favorite celebrity. **A**	Write about the rules of your favorite sport or game. **B**
Write a summary of your favorite book. **C**	Write instructions on how to clean your room. **D**
Interview someone and write about their job. **E**	Write about the types of animals that live in your climate. **F**
Write a description of your hometown for someone who has never been there. **G**	Write a description of your state for someone who has never been there. **H**

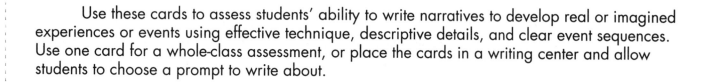

Use these cards to assess students' ability to write narratives to develop real or imagined experiences or events using effective technique, descriptive details, and clear event sequences. Use one card for a whole-class assessment, or place the cards in a writing center and allow students to choose a prompt to write about.

One day, a spaceship lands on the playground at your school. Write to tell what happens next. **A**	Write a story about a day when everything goes wrong. **B**
Imagine waking up and finding that you had switched places with your pet dog or cat. What would you do? Write a story of your day as a dog or cat. **C**	Imagine having a car that could take you anywhere you wanted for one day. Where would you go? Write a story about that day. **D**
Write a story about what it would be like if you woke up one morning with wings. **E**	Write a story about what you would do with a million dollars. **F**
Think about a trip you went on with your class, family, friends, or a group. Write about what happened on the trip. **G**	Imagine something extraordinary happened to you. Write to tell about it. **H**

Research Project
Writing Prompts

Use these cards to assess students' ability to conduct short research projects that use several sources to build knowledge through investigation of different aspects of a topic. Use one card for a whole-class assessment, or place the cards in a writing center and allow students to choose a prompt to write about.

Research and write about what life may be like inside a beehive. **A**	Research and write about the Olympics in ancient Greece. **B**
Research the platypus and write about what makes it an interesting and unique animal. **C**	Research the women's suffrage movement and write about how it changed America. **D**
Research the Lost Colony and write about the possible explanations. **E**	Research the importance of sleep and write about your findings. **F**
Research your state and write about what makes it unique. **G**	Research the history of transportation and write about how railroads changed life in America. **H**

Editing and Revising

Rewrite each paragraph, correcting all of the mistakes in conventions and grammar.

1. bryan went to the beech last weekend. he goed with his family. bryan builded a giant sand castle with his brother. he swimmed to. bryan really enjoys his trip

_____

_____

_____

2. im so excited about Camping this summer? we is going fishing and swiming two. my favrite part is sleeping under the stars. I no we will have so much fun.

_____

_____

_____

3. deer aunt hazel
    I ca'nt weight to sea you next month. I have sew many things planned for your visit. Dont forget to bring you're towel goggles and suit? We will spent most of are time at the lake!
love
your nefew

_____

_____

_____

_____

Combine the following sentences by joining them with a conjunction.

4. The phone was ringing. I answered it.

_____

5. It's time for dinner. I am not hungry.

_____

6. We cannot run in the hallway. We cannot talk in the hallway.

_____

Write one opinion about today's lesson.

_____

List at least three details to support your opinion.

- _____
- _____
- _____

A

Explain the difference between narrative and explanatory writing.

_____
_____
_____
_____
_____

B

If you could research anything, what would you want to learn more about?

_____

List three references where you could find more information about your topic.

- _____
- _____
- _____

C

Develop a personal narrative prompt and an imaginative narrative prompt.

_____
_____
_____
_____
_____

D

Who read your writing today?

_____

What suggestions did he/she give you?

_____
_____
_____
_____

E

List linking/transition words and phrases that will help when writing an informative piece.

_____
_____
_____
_____
_____

F

List linking/transition words and phrases that will help when writing an opinion piece.

_____
_____
_____
_____
_____

G

How did you organize your writing?

_____

Why did you organize it this way?

_____
_____
_____
_____

H

✦ Show What You Know ✦
Grammar and Conventions

Circle the conjunction, preposition, or interjection in each sentence. Then, write **C** for conjunction, **P** for preposition, or **I** for interjection.

_____   **1.** Ouch, that hurt!

_____   **2.** Please place this behind the table.

_____   **3.** It is raining so we can't go.

Circle the correctly written sentence in each pair.

4. Don plays neither baseball nor basketball.

Don neither plays baseball nor basketball.

5. Eddie has practiced five extra hours this week.

Eddie had practiced five extra hours this week.

6. When I was, young I will swim every day of the summer.

When I was young, I would swim every day of the summer.

Rewrite the following passages correctly. Correct all capitalization, punctuation, spelling, and verb tense errors.

7. tomorrow we will left for the beach i was so excited. i can't weight to fill the sand on my toes my brothers are already their we had so much fun

_____

_____

8. they're are so many reasons too love turtles first they are so cute. turtles are smart two. I wish my mom will let me have won as a pet.

_____

_____

Name _____ Date _____

✦ Show What You Know ✦
Grammar and Conventions

Circle the conjunction, preposition, or interjection in each sentence. Then, write **C** for conjunction, **P** for preposition, or **I** for interjection.

_____ **1.** The shop is near the bus station.

_____ **2.** Would you rather chop the onions or peel the potatoes?

_____ **3.** Ahh, you scared me!

Circle the correctly written sentence in each pair.

4. We can either eat now or after the show.

We can eat now or either after the show.

5. Mark enjoys attending the play last night.

Mark enjoyed attending the play last night.

6. Tomorrow, I will return the book.

Tomorrow, I returned the book.

Rewrite the following passages correctly. Correct all capitalization, punctuation, spelling, and verb tense errors.

7. as soon as i arrived i knew something was wrong? the lights were off, and their always own. i flipped the switch and were surprised to see all my friends and family

_____

_____

_____

8. i couldn't weight any longer. I tore the rapping off of my last present. finally my wish had come true I throwed my arms around there necks and hug as tight as I could

_____

_____

_____

✦ Show What You Know
Vocabulary

Complete the chart.

	Affix	Meaning	Example
1.	non-		
2.	pre-		
3.		opposite of	
4.	tri-		
5.		half	

Match each term with its definition.

_____ **6.** two words spelled the same but have different meanings

_____ **7.** a short saying, stating a general truth or piece of advice

_____ **8.** a figure of speech in which two unlike things are compared directly

_____ **9.** an alphabetical list of words and their definitions located at the back of a text

_____ **10.** a word or phrase that is not taken literally

_____ **11.** a figure of speech in which two unlike things are compared using the words *like* or *as*

_____ **12.** a word or phrase that means exactly or nearly the same as another word or phrase.

_____ **13.** a book that lists words and their synonyms

_____ **14.** a word or phrase opposite in meaning to another word or phrase

_____ **15.** a book or electronic resource that lists words alphabetically and gives their meaning

A. dictionary

B. glossary

C. thesaurus

D. simile

E. metaphor

F. idiom

G. proverb/adage

H. synonym

I. antonym

J. homographs

✦ Show What You Know
Vocabulary

Complete the chart.

	Affix	Meaning	Example
1.	inter-		
2.	ex-		
3.			microscope
4.	-ful		
5.			fearless

Match each term with its example.

_____ **6.** cry; pout

_____ **7.** It is raining cats and dogs!

_____ **8.** excited; depressed

_____ **9.** a flying mammal and a wooden club used to hit a ball

_____ **10.** Jan used the back of her science text to look up the term *photosynthesis*.

_____ **11.** She looked as white as a ghost!

_____ **12.** I directed Kathy to use this book to look up several words she didn't know.

_____ **13.** Her tears were a river flowing down her cheeks.

_____ **14.** Darrell used a book to find synonyms to replace some of the words in his report.

_____ **15.** Where there's smoke, there's fire.

A. dictionary

B. glossary

C. thesaurus

D. simile

E. metaphor

F. idiom

G. proverb/adage

H. synonyms

I. antonyms

J. homographs

Name _____ Date _____

Conjunctions, Prepositions, and Interjections

Circle the conjunction, preposition, or interjection in each sentence. Then, write **C** for conjunction, **P** for preposition, or **I** for interjection.

_____ **1.** Ow! I have a toothache!

_____ **2.** There are three books on the table.

_____ **3.** Shh! We're taking a test!

_____ **4.** I woke up because I was thirsty.

_____ **5.** We could go to the movies, or we could go to the park.

_____ **6.** Wow! That was an incredible show!

_____ **7.** He put the dishes in the sink.

_____ **8.** Although he wanted to attend the concert, he could not find a ticket.

_____ **9.** Yikes, I'm sorry!

_____ **10.** Keith cannot eat peanuts because he is allergic to them.

_____ **11.** Meet us at the park.

_____ **12.** Oh, I forgot to bring my glove!

_____ **13.** We went to a campground that had a pool.

_____ **14.** The dog hid under the bed.

Circle the sentence that uses correlative conjunctions correctly.

15. Neither I know Jim nor Bob very well.   I know neither Jim nor Bob very well.

16. Either I will bake or fry the potatoes.   I will either bake or fry the potatoes.

17. I would rather drink water than milk.   I rather would drink water than milk.

18. I was nervous and both excited before   I was both nervous and excited before the
the championship game.   championship game.

Name _____ Date _____

Verb Tense

Choose the best answer.

1. The car _____ fine since we changed the oil.
   A. had worked
   B. has worked
   C. will have worked
   D. have worked

2. We _____ too much sugar today.
   A. has eaten
   B. will ate
   C. will have eat
   D. have eaten

Circle the verb tense used in each sentence.

3. I carry my book bag with me to school everyday.

        past   present   future

4. Our class solves problems every day.

        past   present   future

5. This summer, we will visit the Grand Canyon.

        past   present   future

6. His family exercises together every afternoon.

        past   present   future

7. The dog barked at the mail carrier.

        past   present   future

8. Rewrite the following paragraph to correct any incorrect shifts in verb tense.

    We went to the waterpark last week. It is a lot of fun! We will ride all of the water slides! We stand in line for the Lazy River, but not for too long. We had fun, but we are exhausted!

_____

_____

_____

_____

_____

Name _____ Date _____

Capitalization and Punctuation

Rewrite the following sentences correctly. Add commas, capitalization, and ending punctuation. Also, correctly indicate any titles of works.

1. yes I will go to the game tonight

_____

2. is it cold katie

_____

3. when I went to the mall I bought a new shirt

_____

4. will you pick up milk eggs and bread on your way home

_____

5. it was a beautiful day so we went to the park

_____

6. this is an important meeting for you isn't it

_____

7. the short sweet lady standing in the back is my grandmother

_____

8. when it stops raining we can go swimming

_____

9. the magazine baking on a budget just arrived at our house

_____

10. my dog and me is a great book

_____

Name _____ Date _____

Spelling

Write the correct spelling for each word.

1. plural form of army _____

2. plural form of half _____

3. plural form of hero _____

4. past tense of chop _____

5. past tense of cry _____

6. plural form of self _____

Write the comparative and superlative forms for each adjective. (i.e. big, bigger, biggest)

7. steady, _____, _____

8. young, _____, _____

9. busy, _____, _____

10. simple, _____, _____

Circle the correct spelling for each word.

11. (There, Their, They're) on (there, their, they're) way now.

12. Don't forget (you're, your) jacket.

13. (There, Their, They're) are not that many left.

14. (You're, Your) the best!

15. (Were, Where, We're) going to be late!

Use these cards to assess students' understanding of affixes. You may choose to have a student match each affix with its meaning. Or, present a student with a prefix or suffix and have him identify and define a word using that affix. For a more informal assessment, all cards can be distributed to the class so that students can find their matches. Students could also play a memory game with the cards.

un- **A**	again **B**
pre- **C**	wrongly **D**
-less **E**	resembling **F**
-able **G**	state or quality of **H**

dis- **I**	not, into **J**
non- **K**	not, opposite of **L**
in- **M**	mis- **N**
not, opposite of **O**	before **P**
re- **Q**	not, opposite of **R**

-ful <div align="right">**S**</div>	without <div align="right">**T**</div>
-ness <div align="right">**U**</div>	is, can be <div align="right">**V**</div>
one who <div align="right">**W**</div>	-er <div align="right">**X**</div>
-est <div align="right">**Y**</div>	full of <div align="right">**Z**</div>
-ly <div align="right">**AA**</div>	most (when comparing) <div align="right">**AB**</div>

Name _____   Date _____

Using Reference Materials

Use the dictionary entry to answer questions 1–4.

> **record** (ri′kôrd) v. **1.** to put something into a lasting form, such as writing or film **2.** to make a note of something
> **record** (′rekərd) n. **3.** an account of something, set in writing or other form **4.** a piece of music on a disc

Write the number of the correct definition for how the word **record** is used in each sentence.

1. Do you have a **record** of the payment? _____

2. He was able to **record** all of the ceremony. _____

3. Please **record** that in your journal. _____

4. The band's latest **record** came out last fall. _____

5. Which word would you find on the dictionary page with the following guide words?

hair	happy

   A. hare   B. hammock   C. hardly   D. hay

6. Which word would you find on the dictionary page with the following guide words?

crass	credible

   A. crabby   B. careful   C. creative   D. cross

Determine which would be the most appropriate reference material for each sentence. Write **D** for dictionary, **G** for glossary, and **T** for thesaurus.

_____ **7.** Jenny used a word too many times in her report, and she'd like to replace several of the duplicates without changing the meaning.

_____ **8.** Carl is unsure of the meaning of several words in the novel he's reading.

_____ **9.** Brandon needs help making vocabulary flash cards so he can study for his science test.

_____ **10.** Lori needs to find out if a particular word has more than one meaning.

Similes and Metaphors

Identify each description as a simile or a metaphor by writing **S** for simile or **M** for metaphor. Then, write the two things that are being compared on the lines.

1. _____ Hannah runs like the wind.

_____   _____

2. _____ My mom is as pretty as a flower.

_____   _____

3. _____ Books are her vacation.

_____   _____

4. _____ Donny is a fish when he swims.

_____   _____

5. _____ His stomach is a bottomless pit.

_____   _____

Identify each description as a simile or metaphor by writing **S** for a simile or **M** for a metaphor. Then, explain the meaning of the comparison.

6. _____ The wind was like a piercing arrow.

_____

7. _____ Her eyes were as big as saucers after she heard the news.

_____

8. _____ Those girls are two peas in a pod.

_____

9. _____ Katie swims like a fish!

_____

10. _____ He is a cheetah on the track!

_____

Similes and Metaphors

Use these cards to assess general understanding of similes and metaphors. Have a student sort the cards into similes and metaphors. Additionally, you may choose to have her identify the two things being compared or explain the meaning of a simile or metaphor. If desired, laminate the cards to allow students to use write-on/wipe-away markers to circle the two things being compared. As students progress with figurative language, encourage them to make their own cards to add to the sorts.

This morning, I feel as fresh as a daisy. **A**	The horse's mane was black as coal. **B**
His room is a pigpen. **C**	The dark, cold, and silent room was a tomb. **D**
That baby is as cute as a button. **E**	She has a heart of gold. **F**
I'm as hungry as a bear that just awoke from hibernation. **G**	My feet are as cold as ice. **H**

She was as quiet as a mouse.

I

He was as strong as an ox.

J

My brother is a pig
when he eats.

K

Even though she was anxious,
she appeared as cool
as a cucumber.

L

We decided to be couch
potatoes all day.

M

You are the light of my life.

N

He felt as slow as a snail during
his first marathon.

O

He has the heart of a lion.

P

The teacher was as
tough as nails.

Q

His plans were as solid
as a rock.

R

Name _____   Date _____

Idioms, Adages, and Proverbs

Circle the idiom in each sentence. Then, explain its meaning.

1. He tried not to let the cat out of the bag, but ended up accidentally telling his mom about her surprise party.

_____

2. The phone call from her childhood friend came out of the blue.

_____

3. Tommy, stop beating around the bush and just tell me what happened.

_____

4. Mom said that I would play basketball until the cows came home if she let me.

_____

5. Jeff's mom was under the weather so she didn't make it to the game.

_____

Explain the meaning of each proverb or adage.

6. Don't judge a book by its cover.

_____

7. All that glitters is not gold.

_____

8. Out of sight, out of mind.

_____

9. Every cloud has a silver lining.

_____

10. The pen is mightier than the sword.

_____

Name _____ Date _____

Synonyms and Antonyms

Write **S** if the words are synonyms. Write **A** if the words are antonyms.

1. tired, energetic _____   **2.** noisy, quiet _____   **3.** estimate, guess _____

4. huge, gigantic _____   **5.** windy, calm _____   **6.** drowsy, sleepy _____

Write a synonym for each word.

7. tiny _____   **8.** thin _____   **9.** stinky _____

10. smile _____   **11.** friendly _____   **12.** delicious _____

Write an antonym for each word.

13. large _____   **14.** sprint _____   **15.** bright _____

16. cry _____   **17.** sunny _____   **18.** exhausted _____

Write a synonym and antonym for each word.

		Synonym	**Antonym**
19.	damp		
20.	wealthy		
21.	hungry		
22.	build		
23.	sick		
24.	hard		
25.	primary		

Homographs

Write two sentences for each homograph, using a different meaning in each sentence.

1. bat

_____

_____

2. duck

_____

_____

3. pitcher

_____

_____

4. can

_____

_____

5. fly

_____

_____

Use the word bank to write the homograph that matches the definitions.

bank	bark	bow	tear	wave

6. _____ the front of a ship; a ribbon on a gift or in someone's hair

7. _____ the sound a dog makes; the outer layer of a tree

8. _____ fluid that comes from the eye; to rip something

9. _____ to move one's hand to and fro in greeting or as a signal; a long body of water curling into an arched form

10. _____ a financial institution that people or businesses can keep their money in or borrow money from; a raised area of land along the side of a river.

A

Complete the sentences with the correct correlative conjunction.

Both Bactrian camels _____ Arabian camels can carry heavy loads.

You can **neither** go by bus _____ by taxi.

We can go to _____ the mountains **or** the beach for vacation.

B

Circle the prepositions.

Patrick walked around the block three times.

He moved the sign across the street.

We could hear yelling just outside the office.

C

Underline the interjection in each sentence.

Ahh, now I see what you mean.

Shh! The movie is about to start!

Wow, that is really great news!

D

Complete the sentences using the correct tense of the verb **arrive**.

The packages _____ late last week.

Hopefully, they _____ before the show starts.

They plan to _____ at 1:00 pm sharp.

E

Complete the sentence using the correct tense of the verb **ring**.

The bell _____ loud and clear early this morning.

She _____ the doorbell more than once if they do not answer.

_____ the bell on your way out if you were happy with your meal.

F

Rewrite the sentences with correct capitalization and punctuation.

i really wanted ms greer for fifth grade

who did she go with to the movies

he traveled to canada last summer to visit his nephew joseph

G

Rewrite each sentence on another sheet of paper. Add commas where needed.

He ate toast eggs and fruit for breakfast.

Are you in there Dan?

If you are late you won't be able to see the movie.

H

Rewrite the following sentences correctly, indicating any titles. Add commas where needed.

He received his last monthly edition of campers' world in the mail.

The TV show a girl's life airs at four o'clock this afternoon.

She was excited that her favorite book jessica's anthem was going to be a movie!

I

Write a synonym and an antonym for each.

soft _____ _____

rough _____ _____

sour _____ _____

separate _____ _____

J

Past Tense	Present Tense	Future Tense
loved		
	take	
		will fly

K

Write **S** for simile, **M** for metaphor, **I** for idiom, and **P** for proverb.

_____ cool as a cucumber

_____ actions speak louder than words

_____ life is a highway

_____ raining cats and dogs

L

Prefix/Suffix	Meaning	Example

M

Match the following reference materials to their definitions.

1. dictionary   A. a book with synonyms listed for each word

2. thesaurus   B. located in the back of textbook with key content vocabulary

3. glossary   C. a book with definitions listed for each word

N

Figurative Language Example	Type	Meaning

O

Spell the following misspelled words correctly. Then, use each in a sentence.

trycycle _____

probly _____

alot _____

themselfs _____

P

Choose the correct word to complete each sentence.

(Their, There, They're) going to be our new neighbors!

Please do not leave (your, you're) shoes on the porch.

They (we're, were) not leaving until Saturday.

Answer Key

Pages 9–10

1. playing the guitar, performing; 2. C; 3. A; 4. B; 5. metaphor, The author is trying to illustrate that the narrator is nervous. 6. A; 7. Answers will vary. 8. courage and facing fears, The narrator was scared and nervous but got on stage and performed anyway. 9. nervous at the beginning, narrator refers to the butterflies in her stomach, proud and happy at the end, she was smiling after the performance; 10. C

Pages 11–12

1. A; 2. third person; 3. They love animals and have rescued many animals growing up. 4. B; 5. a veterinarian, Their dad asked who's going to provide medical attention. It also mentions that the twins will be cleaning out kennels at his office. 6. C; 7. idiom, The twins are super excited and pleased that their parents agreed. 8. hard work and preparedness are valuable, The twins worked hard planning. 9. Answers will vary.

Pages 13–14

A. school; B. library; C. camping; D. planting a garden; E. birthday party; F. grocery store; G. doctor's office; H. zoo; I. baseball game; J. baking; K. recess, to play; L. swimming; M. It got a flat tire. N. taking a test

Page 15

1. Yes, because she left the experience section empty. 2. No, because she was able to give Hayley advice and explain what was going to happen. 3. No, because she wore flip-flops and didn't know anything about the dance portion.

Page 16

1. C; 2. at the DMV, to get his license, Answers will vary. 3. A; 4. the car keys, He talks about filling up the tank. 5. He was excited. He ran out of the building with a huge grin.

Page 17

1. playing baseball, Answers will vary. 2. He was nervous. Answers will vary. 3. nervous and scared, then happy and proud; 4. He cost the team an out. A team gets penalized with an out if a batter gets three strikes. 5. Answers will vary.

Page 18

1. honesty; 2. cooperation; 3. courage; 4. acceptance; 5. hope; 6. kindness; 7. friendship; 8. compassion; 9. preparedness; 10. perseverance

Page 19

1. A; 2. B, C; 3. C; 4. to do better than expected, Ethan scored 100 percent on his test, which is better than his goal of 95 percent.

Page 20

1. perseverance; 2. Answers will vary. 3. barely touched, Answers will vary. 4. Answers will vary.

Page 21

1. The boys live in the same neighborhood, are in the same class, and both excel at something. 2. Brayden is studious and kind. Reid is athletic and hurts others' feelings. 3. A. brightest, studious, diligent, took pride in academic achievements; B. best athlete, competitive, enjoyed winning; 4. He probably thought they didn't have anything in common but was very thankful for him and his kindness at the end. Check students' work.

Answer Key

Page 22

1. At first, she was nervous and scared. She was dreading camp. By the end, she didn't want to leave. She made lots of new friends and had lots of fun. Answers will vary. 2. She'll probably ask her mom to attend camp again because she had so much fun. Answers will vary. 3. On Day 1, she was afraid of heights and scared to sleep on the top bunk. Zip line and ropes course are both activities that are high up.

Page 23

1. simile, It compares two unlike things using *like* or *as*. 2. She felt really sick. She was scared and nervous since she had not swam since last year. 3. swimming; Elizabeth said she would help her practice swimming. 4. She blushed because she was embarrassed. She was embarrassed that she was scared to go in the deep end.

Page 24

1. simile, It compares two unlike things using *like* or *as*. It means he runs fast. 2. hyperbole, He's exaggerating the quantity of food he eats. It means he eats a lot. 3. metaphor, It compares two unlike things directly. It means he is kind. 4. He stays on the couch and is lazy all day. 5. Check students' work.

Page 25

A. third; B. first; C. first; D. third; E. third; F. third; G. first; H. first

Page 26

1. B; 2. The "I" in the passage walked to school with Josh, was in the same class, and ate lunch with him. 3. gonna, yeah right, are you kiddin' me, you're sure havin' a sweet day; The author used this language to portray the language of young boys. 4. Check students' work.

Pages 27–28

A. basketball, Answers will vary. B. quilt, blanket, Answers will vary. C. Answers will vary. D. 3rd, Answers will vary. E. 1st, Answers will vary. F. book–chapter, drama–act, poem–stanza; G–I. Answers will vary. K. first, third, first; L–M. Answers will vary. N. metaphor, Answers will vary. O. metaphor, Answers will vary. P. simile, Answers will vary.

Pages 29–30

1. No one is quite sure who was the first to invent the beloved ice-cream cone. Answers will vary. 2. B; 3. They both improvised and created an ice-cream cone. 4. Marchiony's first cone was actually made of paper. He created it because his glass dishes were getting broken or lost. Menches ran out of dishes. He used his friend's pastries instead. 5. D; 6. C; 7. People were breaking or taking his dishes. 8. someone that sells something; The passage talks about Menches being a vendor and having a stand on the street to sell ice cream.

Pages 31–32

1. Camels are used to transport things and were suited to their jobs. 2. C; 3. Both can carry heavy loads and can store fat and water. 4. The Bactrian is sturdier, has two humps, and can withstand cooler climates. The Arabian camel has shorter hair and has one hump. 5. A; 6. B; 7. Answers will vary but may include that they sway back and forth like ships on the water and they carry cargo to and from places like ships. 8. To move things from one place to another.

Answer Key

Page 33

1. People killed elephants for their ivory.
2. They would be extinct. Answers will vary.
3. Their population will continue to grow. Answers will vary. 4. help, ease; Answers will vary. 5. Large companies refused to buy ivory. Laws were then passed banning the sale of ivory so there was no need to kill the elephants any more.

Page 34

1. A; 2. B, C; 3. Answers will vary. 4. Answers will vary but should include cold-blooded vs. warm-blooded, body coverings, habitats, reproduction, and types of breathing.

Page 35

1. SD, T, MI, SD; 2. MI, SD, T, SD; 3. T, SD, SD, MI; 4. MI, T, SD, SD; 5. SD, MI, SD, T

Page 36

1. viral infectious disease; 2. epidemic;
3. It spreads quickly and lasts a long time.
4. The plague is an example. 5. pandemic;
6. It spreads across the world. 7. Smallpox is an example. 8. endemic; 9. It occurs in a certain area or population. 10. Malaria is an example.

Page 37

1. C; 2. to light up; 3. Topic: moon phases; Main Idea: The phases of the moon are caused by the part of the moon that is lit by the sun. Supporting Details: As the moon rotates around Earth, the moon is illuminated by light from the sun. It takes about 29.5 days for our moon to cycle through all of the phases. 4. D;
5. Answers will vary.

Page 38

1. A; 2–3. Answers will vary. 4. sail all the way around something; 5. Check students' work.

Pages 39–40

1. B; 2. slavery, women, rights; 3. Check students' work. 4. Answers will vary.

Page 41

1. C; 2. B; 3. B; 4–5. Answers will vary.

Page 42

1. Answers will vary. 2. C; 3. C;
4–5. Answers will vary.

Page 43

1. a grilled cheese sandwich; 2. C; 3. B;
4. pan, The recipe says to place skillet on burner on medium heat. 5. C

Page 44

1. Mount Vesuvius, Answers will vary. 2. Both were composite volcanoes and affected large areas. 3. The people had no warning at Mount Vesuvius. 4. D; 5–6. Answers will vary.

Page 46

1. a day in the life on the farm; 2. enjoys farming, Answers will vary. 3. does not enjoy farming, Answers will vary. 4. Answers will vary.

Pages 47–48

A–P. Answers will vary.

Answer Key

Page 61

The Dilemma

1. tired; 2. All work and no play is not healthy.
3. He was excited about all of his possible adventures. 4. third person

The Water Park

1. Answers will vary. 2. The boys don't have enough money to go to the water park. 3. They earn money by doing chores. 4. their house

Light Show in the Sky

1. They were excited for what was about to happen. 2. outside; 3. looking at the sky;
4. because they saw the northern lights and were amazed

Whales

1. to breathe; 2. to help keep them warm, to help them stay afloat; 3. a filter whales use to trap food; 4. for their blubber

The Truth About History

1. because they were written by different people in the cities where the teams were from;
2. because we didn't witness it; 3. causing debate; 4. Answers will vary.

Blink of an Eye

1. damaged; 2. Answers will vary. 3. kept moist; 4. 15,000 times a day

Page 64

A–B. Answers will vary. C. shelves, trophies, weird, Answers will vary. D. pre–before, less–without, un–not, opposite of, re–again, Answers will vary. E. Answers will vary.
F. gave, known, swim; G–H. Answers will vary.

Page 69

1. Bryan went to the beach last weekend with his family. Bryan built a giant sand castle with his brother. He swam too. Bryan really enjoyed his trip! 2. I'm so excited about camping this summer! We are going fishing and swimming too. My favorite part is sleeping under the stars. I know we will have so much fun. 3. Dear Aunt Hazel, I can't wait to see you next month. I have so many things planned for your visit.

Don't forget to bring your towel, goggles, and suit. We will spend most of our time at the lake! Love, Your Nephew; 4. The phone was ringing so I answered it. 5. It's time for dinner but I am not hungry. 6. We cannot run or talk in the hallway.

Page 70

A–H. Answers will vary.

Page 71

1. Ouch, I; 2. behind, P; 3. so, C; 4. Don plays neither baseball nor basketball. 5. Eddie has practiced five extra hours this week.
6. When I was young, I would swim every day of the summer. 7. Tomorrow, we will leave for the beach. I am so excited! I can't wait to feel the sand on my toes. My brothers are already there. We will have so much fun! 8. There are so many reasons to love turtles. First, they are so cute! Turtles are smart too. I wish my mom would let me have one as a pet.

Page 72

1. near, P; 2. or, C; 3. Ahh, I; 4. We can either eat now or after the show. 5. Mark enjoyed attending the play last night. 6. Tomorrow, I will return the book. 7. As soon as I arrived, I knew something was wrong. The lights were off, and they're always on. I flipped the switch and was surprised to see all my friends and family! 8. I couldn't wait any longer. I tore the wrapping off of my last present. Finally, my wish had come true! I threw my arms around their necks and hugged as tight as I could.

Page 73

1. not, opposite of, Answers will vary.
2. before, Answers will vary. 3. *dis-*, opposite of; 4. three, Answers will vary. 5. *semi-*, Answers will vary. 6. J; 7. G; 8. E; 9. B; 10. F; 11. D; 12. H; 13. C; 14. I; 15. A

Answer Key

Page 74

1. between, Answers will vary. 2. out of, former, Answers will vary. 3. *micro*, small; 4. full of, Answers will vary. 5. *-less*, without; 6. H; 7. F; 8. I; 9. J; 10. B; 11. D; 12. A; 13. E; 14. C; 15. G

Page 75

1. Ow, I; 2. on, P; 3. Shh, I; 4. because, C; 5. or, C; 6. wow, I; 7. in, P; 8. although, C; 9. Yikes, I; 10, because, C; 11. at, P; 12. Oh, I; 13. that, C; 14. under; P; 15. I know neither Jim nor Bob very well. 16. I will either bake or fry the potatoes. 17. I would rather drink water than milk. 18. I was both nervous and excited before the championship game.

Page 76

1. B; 2. D; 3. present; 4. present; 5. future; 6. present; 7. past; 8. We went to the waterpark last week. It was a lot of fun! We rode all of the water slides! We stood in line for the Lazy River, but not for too long. We had fun, but we were exhausted!

Page 77

1. Yes, I will go to the game tonight. 2. Is it cold, Katie? 3. When I went to the mall, I bought a new shirt. 4. Will you pick up milk, eggs, and bread on your way home? 5. It was a beautiful day, so we went to the park. 6. This is an important meeting for you, isn't it? 7. The short, sweet lady standing in the back is my grandmother. 8. When it stops raining, we can go swimming. 9. The magazine *Baking on a Budget* just arrived at our house. 10. *My Dog and Me* is a great book.

Page 78

1. armies; 2. halves; 3. heroes; 4. chopped; 5. cried; 6. selves; 7. steadier, steadiest; 8. younger, youngest; 9. busier, busiest; 10. simpler, simplest; 11. They're, their;

12. your; 13. There; 14. You're; 15. We're

Page 82

1. 3; 2. 1; 3. 2; 4. 4; 5. B; 6. C; 7. T; 8. D; 9. G; 10. D

Page 83

1. S, Hannah's running, the wind; 2. S, mom, flower; 3. M, books, vacation; 4. M, Donny, fish; 5. M, stomach, bottomless pit; 6. S, The wind was really strong. 7. S, Her eyes were really big because she was surprised. 8. M, They get along well and are always together. 9. S, Katie swims really well. 10. M, He's a super fast runner.

Page 86

1. let the cat out of the bag, telling something that wasn't supposed to be told; 2. out of the blue, it was unexpected; 3. beating around the bush, not getting to the point; 4. until the cows came home, for a really long time; 5. under the weather, sick; 6. Don't judge something or someone based on appearance. 7. Just because something looks or sounds good does not necessarily mean that it is good. 8. Something is more easily forgotten or dismissed as unimportant if it is not in our direct view. 9. You can find something good in every bad situation. 10. Trying to convince people with ideas and words is more effective than trying to force people to do what you want.

Page 87

1. A; 2. A; 3. S; 4. S; 5. A; 6. S; Answers will vary but may include: 7. little; 8. skinny; 9. smelly; 10. grin; 11. nice; 12. tasty; 13. small; 14. walk; 15. dull; 16. laugh; 17. cloudy; 18. energized; 19. moist, dry; 20. rich, poor; 21. starving, full; 22. construct, destroy; 23. ill, well; 24. solid, soft; 25. first, secondary

Answer Key

Page 88

1–5. Answers will vary. 6. bow; 7. bark;
8. tear; 9. wave; 10. bank

Pages 89–90

A. and, nor, either; B. around, across, outside;
C. Ahh, Shh, Wow; D. arrived, will arrive,
arrive; E. rang, will ring, Ring; F. I really
wanted Ms. Greer for fifth grade. Who did she
go with to the movies? He traveled to Canada
last summer to visit his nephew, Joseph.
G. He ate toast, eggs, and fruit for breakfast.
Are you in there, Dan? If you are late, you
won't be able to see the movie. H. He received
his last monthly edition of *Campers' World* in
the mail. The TV show *A Girl's Life* airs at four
o'clock this afternoon. She was excited that her
favorite book, *Jessica's Anthem*, was going to
be a movie! Answers will vary but may include:
I. fluffy–hard, bumpy–smooth,
tart–sweet, divide–combine; J. love, will
love, took, will take, flew, fly; K. S, P, M, I;
L. Answers will vary. M. 1. C, 2. A, 3. B; N.
Answers will vary. O. tricycle, probably, a lot,
themselves, Answers will vary. P. They're, your,
were